the social side
of politics

the society pages

the social side
of politics

douglas hartmann
UNIVERSITY OF MINNESOTA

christopher uggen
UNIVERSITY OF MINNESOTA

w. w. norton & company
NEW YORK | LONDON

W. W. Norton & Company has been independent since its founding in 1923, when William Warder Norton and Mary D. Herter Norton first published lectures delivered at the People's Institute, the adult education division of New York City's Cooper Union. The firm soon expanded its program beyond the Institute, publishing books by celebrated academics from America and abroad. By mid-century, the two major pillars of Norton's publishing program—trade books and college texts—were firmly established. In the 1950s, the Norton family transferred control of the company to its employees, and today—with a staff of four hundred and a comparable number of trade, college, and professional titles published each year—W. W. Norton & Company stands as the largest and oldest publishing house owned wholly by its employees.

Book Design: Isaac Tobin
Composition: Westchester Book Composition
Manufacturing: Courier-Westford
Production Manager: Sean Mintus

ISBN: 978-0-393-92037-6

W. W. Norton & Company, Inc., 500 Fifth Avenue, New York, NY 10110-0017
www.wwnorton.com
W. W. Norton & Company, Ltd., Castle House, 75/76 Wells Street, London
W1T3QT

contents

part 3 critical takes 143

series preface

DOUGLAS HARTMANN AND CHRISTOPHER UGGEN

I t started with a conversation about record labels. Our favorite imprints are known for impeccable taste, creative design, and an eye for quality and originality. Wouldn't it be cool if W. W. Norton and TheSocietyPages.org joined forces to develop a book series with the same goals in mind? Namely, we set out to consistently deliver the best work by the most original voices in the field, online and, now, in your hands.

The Society Pages (TSP) is a multidisciplinary, online hub bringing fresh social scientific knowledge and insight to the broadest public audiences in the most open, accessible, and timely manner possible. The largest, most visible collection of sociological material on the Web (currently drawing over one million hits per month), TSP is composed of a family of prolific Community Pages (blogs and bloggers), original features, peer-reviewed white papers, podcasts, interviews, teaching content, and new and classic reading recommendations. Now our TSP volumes assemble the best of this original content in key thematic collections. With contributions from leading scholars, insights from influential voices (including Lisa Wade and Gwen Sharp's wildly popular Community Page Sociological Images), and a provocative collection of discussion topics and group activities, this innovative new series will provide an accessible and affordable entry point for strong sociological perspectives on topics of immediate relevance for a new generation of social media-savvy readers.

This first volume focuses on politics. Drawn largely from feature content, posts, and exchanges provoked by the elections of 2012, the chapters are organized in a way that exemplifies the three signature sections of the books to come. In this instance, "Core Contributions" features articles that demonstrate how sociologists and other social scientists think about otherwise familiar political phenomena like power, polling, and social movements. Chapters in the "Cultural Contexts" section draw out the political content and implication of cultural realms—from religion and race to sports, humor, and new media technologies—that are often ignored or taken for granted. The "Critical Takes" rubric then gathers pieces that provide sociological commentary, perspective, and reflection. In this volume, this section's focus is on inequalities embedded in and reproduced through the political system (especially in the case of race, which has been such a prominent issue in the Obama era), how sociological tools and insights are employed in the public sphere, and the role of government in shaping society through public policy.

Each of these concise, accessible chapters reflects The Society Pages' distinctive voice, tone, and style. As with forthcoming volumes in the series, this collection features contributions from Social Facts editor Deborah Carr and the Changing Lenses Project (a collaboration between Hartmann and award-winning documentary photographer Wing Young Huie). Sprinkled throughout, you will find TSP Tie-Ins from our Community Pages, including Cyborgology, Graphic Sociology, and Sociological Images. And the volume concludes with a Discussion Guide and Group Activities page that challenges readers to draw connections among the chapters, think more deeply and critically about politics and its role in their social life, and link content from the book to ongoing conversations and interactive posts online.

introduction

DOUGLAS HARTMANN AND
CHRISTOPHER UGGEN

We didn't plan it this way, but the relaunch of The Society Pages website in partnership with W. W. Norton corresponded with the landmark American elections of 2012. Lucky for us. The campaigns inspired and yielded a veritable treasure trove of political content and postings on our Community Pages and among our contributors. The topics ranged from polling and demographics to the politics of protest and race. So when it came time to assemble the first volume of our new book series, it seemed only natural and timely to focus on politics. This special, first volume of the TSP book series selects the best, most engaging and timely contributions to our site—think of it as our *Greatest Hits Volume I: The Social Side of Politics.*

The biggest challenge of pulling content from the vast sampling of sociological research and commentary available on The Society Pages has come in trying to summarize what is so unique and distinctive about a *sociological* vision of politics. How does this orientation differ from that of other social scientific approaches, particularly those of political science—the scholarly discipline that is explicitly and unambiguously built around the study of "politics"? What is our unique contribution?

In curating the site, working through blog posts, and reviewing and editing submissions, we have learned a great deal about what is unique, powerful, and important about the sociological approach to politics—and how that perspective is put into practice every day on our site. Indeed, one of the great strengths of this volume is that it collects essays on the topics that are the most interesting, important, and timely to the field. In this respect, we believe it provides an extremely useful entree to the field, an entry point to how sociologists think about and research the terrain of the political.

When people think of politics and sociology, the images and ideas that first come to mind are those involving demonstrations, activism, political organizing, and protests. As Steve Buechler's chapter emphasizes, sociologists have been on the leading edge of studying social movements and political activism—from the civil rights movement to union organizing to the Tea Party and Occupy movements. Although we may be a fairly liberal lot, sympathetic to and often involved in protest, the social or perhaps sociological vision of politics goes well beyond social movements and liberal or progressive politics.

Public opinion polling is the most obvious example, but sociologists have contributed to the study of political phenomena by looking at why people vote, how political parties are organized (and organize themselves), and the effects of various "frames" for political issues and candidates. Perhaps most uniquely, political sociologists take a long view toward political issues and how various social and demographic trends affect voting and representation over time. For example, Vincent Roscigno's analysis of power addresses both the structure of institutions like the state and the cultural scaffolding that portrays the status quo as reasonable and justified. Taking power to street-level implementation, Joe Soss and Sarah Shannon discuss the "neoliberal paternalism" guiding contemporary poverty policy as a concrete application of similar themes.

organization

It is these unique, alternative ways of thinking about politics and political processes that constitute the focus of our selections. This volume is organized in three main sections, each of which is intended to highlight distinctive aspects of the sociological vision of and approach to politics.

CORE CONTRIBUTIONS

The first section, "Core Contributions," contains a set of chapters that take a distinctively sociological approach to core concepts and ideas from politics. "Power, Sociologically Speaking," by Vincent Roscigno, exemplifies this approach, revealing how culture and structure combine to create and perpetuate power. A "Roundtable" on polling, curated by Kyle Green, is up next, assembling commentary from three experts in sociological survey work. Social Facts editor Deborah Carr then presents some of the key data around voter registration and turnout; Steven Buechler shows the intimate connections among social movements, politics, and democracy; and Joe R. Feagin offers an unflinching analysis of the pervasive and ongoing racial, even racist structure of the American political system. Feagin's portrayal reflects two key sociological insights about politics: namely, that they are institutional (or based in parties and the apparatus of the state and government) and that such institutions, reflecting the inequalities that structure so much of modern social life, are stubbornly resistant to change.

CULTURAL CONTEXTS

Usually when Americans talk about politics, they are referring to campaigns and elections, legislative debates, and the making of law and public policy. Surely the emphasis on electoral processes represents how much of academic political science is oriented and organized. But there are other, broader aspects of political culture and the impacts of politics—for instance, politics happens in specific social and cultural contexts, affecting domains of life that are rarely thought of as political at all. To get a full picture, we must engage how political communities and interests are created, consolidated, and maintained; political life involves the construction of cultural frames and the identification of which social problems are seen as in need of attention or correction, what is considered core to the public interest, and what's not even worthy of political effort.

In this section, you will read Joe Gerteis's consideration of the historic connections between religion and American political culture—or perhaps even more provocatively, the religious foundations of politics in American life—drawing upon Max Weber's historic visit to the United States. If religion represents the high end of popular culture in America, sports is just as surely seen as its low-brow analog. Kyle Green and Doug Hartmann explore the connections between politics and sport, as well as popular culture and mass media, in their "Strange Bedfellows" piece. With a billion people now using Facebook, Jose Marichal's chapter offers a timely account of how technology is changing and, in some ways, personalizing politics. And while some would say politics is no laughing matter, humor and comedy have long been inter-twined with American political culture. Our TSP Roundtable team helps us understand what's new about Jon Stewart and Stephen Colbert, as well as how they tap into a much longer and storied historical tradition.

These engagements are not always the most tangible or easy to implement in politics or political practice. Indeed, when Green and Hartmann sent a version of their chapter on sport and politics to a left-leaning policy think tank, they were told that it was "interesting" (an ominous term those of us here in Minnesota recognize as among the most pejorative imaginable), but ultimately "too meta." By this, they meant that actual politicians or policymakers would have no use for it, wouldn't know what to do with it. Perhaps. But hope-fully these contributions put a new spin on ultimately politi-cal processes and activities that aren't often recognized as such.

CRITICAL TAKES

A running joke in our TSP board meetings is that sociology is the "Debbie Downer" of the social sciences. Like the main character in the old *Saturday Night Live* skit, the Debbie Down-ers of this world tend to be "glass half empty" all the time. In this way, sociologists are known for picking out our most vexing social problems, documenting the resulting inequalities and their dire social consequences. Is it *all* bad news?

In this volume, we *have* taken on problems. Taking a critical eye to the process, we've assembled several articles about race and politics in the post-2008 era. On the heels of Joe Feagin's system-level analysis in the first section, the first three chapters in this section focus on specific racial dimensions of American politics. The first is Corey Fields's description and analysis of African American Republicanism as a multifaceted, not monolithic, category. Enid Logan's chapter takes a more specific and provocative focus by looking at the role Herman Cain served in the Republican primaries during the 2012 campaign. Rounding out this set, Andra Gillespie considers "The Perils of Transcendence" for postpartisan political figures such as Cory Booker, the African American mayor of Newark, New Jersey, a man who sometimes looks like a real-life superhero (witness his efforts during Hurricane Sandy).

But not all of sociology's "critical takes" involve hand-wringing over persistent inequalities, injustices, and incomplete or incompatible representations. There is, in the critical orientation, also an impulse toward social action and social change. The other two chapters in the section can be read as contributions to this end. Andrew Lindner's treatment of the well-known political pollster and pundit Nate Silver describes how Silver uses sociological tools and concepts in public political commentary, showing how polling and demographics can be used to not only make sense of political developments but also to predict and affect political outcomes and engage audiences. And the volume concludes with an extended interview by Sarah Shannon with Joe Soss, one of the coauthors of an award-winning book on the problems and promise of American welfare policy.

In talking about social policy—both what it is and how we might be able to do it better—Soss and Shannon bring the volume full circle, from discussions of what power is and how it is secured and maintained to how it can be mobilized and used to reproduce the social status quo or to try something a little different. We certainly hope that these articles, taken as a whole, serve that purpose for our readers, helping you not only to understand power and politics but how the political process can be mobilized to remake the social world in which we hope to live.

As always, we should close with our gratitude to the University of Minnesota, W. W. Norton & Company (in particular, the sociology editor, Karl Bakeman), and The Society Pages' graduate student board, many of whom are included as authors in this volume. Hollie Nyseth Brehm has acted as the graduate editor of this volume and, along with Kia Heise, authored the discussion guide and TSP Tie-Ins found throughout. Our associate editor is the incomparable Letta Page.

changing lenses: behind the political process

DOUGLAS HARTMANN WITH WING YOUNG HUIE

Many of the insights and challenges of trying to think about politics in a sociological fashion became clear to our TSP team as we thought about photographs and images to illustrate the many political pieces on our website. The problem with social angles on politics, from a visual point of view, is that the images one might imagine of these contributions tend to be boring (how many pictures of voting booths can you stand?) or too abstract (how would you represent institutional constraints on power?), or the concepts themselves are too big picture (demographic shifts, relationships between religion and political discourse, public policy shifts, etc.) to pin down and represent the moment—much less be of immediate interest or use to politicians, policymakers, or political pundits in the heat of an election season.

© *Wing Young Huie, reprinted with permission.*

At one point, I threw the challenge of visualizing political sociology over to documentary photographer Wing Young Huie as part of our ongoing Changing Lenses project (online at thesocietypages.org/changinglenses). The project is, essentially, a conversation in which, in varying formats, we exchange ideas about what's seen behind a camera lens and what's seen through a sociological lens to get at the diversity of perspectives on the human experience.

Political photographs, Huie admitted, present a bit of a conundrum for him as well. Part of the problem is that he's never been very interested in politics. Also, in his experience, the "circus" surrounding politics is so overwhelming and so orchestrated by media consultants and experts that there is little left to appeal to his artistic sensibilities. Instead, Huie said he tends to be interested in things not usually covered by the political press. "For instance, do aesthetics determine political beliefs or is it the other way around? Why do liberals and conservatives dress the way they do? Can knowing whether or not you like to color outside the lines as a kid be a predictor of your opinion on abortion?" Indeed, Huie summarized—playfully I suspect, perhaps simply for my amusement (since he always reminds me he is *not* a sociologist)—that he tends to be interested in the sociology of politics rather than the politics itself.

From this foundation, we started going through his archive and contact sheets, looking for images that were "political" or "about politics." As expected, it was a bit of a challenge. We found a few images of protests and political rallies. These were fabulous, arresting images, but they carried baggage and political biases. And many of the more sociological images we looked at were difficult to identify as specifically "political." Finally, though, there was one image that we both really locked in on.

This image doesn't have any particular meaning or back-story for Huie. It was on a contact sheet from one of the first rolls he shot for *Frogtown*, the project that really put him on the artistic map. He doesn't have any real memory of the image, the politics, or the event, however. "I think," he explained, "I was just walking around and bumped into it." He goes on: "I only took two shots of the politician, both from the back." Looking at it now, it is "amazing how few of the children, who became unwitting political advertisements, are actually looking at the politician."

But as we continued talking about this picture, we came to realize it was and is a wonderful image and metaphor for the backstage, backstory visions of politics in which we are both interested—images that are not only difficult to represent visually but so often missing from both public and scholarly understandings of politics and the political process. It's a different angle, and one most Americans and American scholars don't usually pay attention to: This, though, is where the action so often missing from both popular and scholarly understandings of politics and the political process really happens.

core contributions

power, sociologically speaking

VINCENT J. ROSCIGNO

A t the close of another hotly contested campaign season, politics seems to me like a sport. We have been
inundated with commercials, bumper stickers,
debates, and speeches. Fans have flaunted their allegiances
while those at the top tried to carve out stances that would
best appeal to particular demographics. Is it worth it? Does
it really matter? What, if anything, really changes because
of all this?

These, of course, are abstract, big-thinking, sociological
kinds of questions. But if I remain uncertain about the
answers, there is one thing that is clearly at stake in all of
this: power. So, what is power? How is it achieved, exercised, and legitimated?

We in the social sciences typically think of power as per-
suasiveness, the ability to get what one wants—this is the
essence of the classic definition attributed to Max Weber,

and it's commonly applied across a host of institutional spheres and interactions, from political parties to the power of consumers. But this view is a bit too simplistic—it obscures power's fundamentally structural, cultural, and relational nature. This is to say, power is too often thought of as something that a particular leader or party has, rather than something rooted in institutional practices, cultural supports, and alternative pathways outside the usual political apparatus.

The problem of power, then, is a prime blind spot; the core, lower-level topics of political science—like individual voting behavior, party politics and alignments, and election outcomes—can direct us away from larger questions about the ends toward which political influence is directed. Sociology is uniquely equipped to look beyond the usual veneer of power, unpack the myths that reinforce it, and see the relational foundations upon which it ultimately rests. A sociological view indeed provides a much-needed corrective, offering a unique glimpse through the myths that veil power's resilience, uses, and limits.

the structured nature of power

As both classic scholars like C. Wright Mills and contemporary sociologists like Cecilia Ridgeway and Lynn Smith-Lovin have made clear, power derives from historically and

the social side of politics

culturally proscribed statuses (such as race and gender) and organizational and institutional positioning (e.g., manager, politician, school administrator). Power is more complex than that, though, as institutional, organizational, and bureaucratic structures confer greater or lesser leverage depending on position. Those of lower status are constrained to playing by the rules much of the time, while those in higher positions might be able to create or use even seemingly neutral rules in self-beneficial ways. Consider how tax codes, exam criteria for college admissions, penalties surrounding "suite" versus "street" crimes, and a bifurcated health-care system benefit the already powerful while creating vulnerabilities and diminishing the power of others. Such arrangements highlight a key sociological insight: Culturally proscribed statuses and positions shape power *and* how that power is enabled or constrained by structure.

Politics and elections, even in an ostensibly democratic system, are not impervious to the structural dynamics of power. One commonly hears, for instance, of the ways in which citizens wield their power through votes. Yet, voting is defined by the structural dictates of law and can be subject to legal or informational manipulation—for instance, gerrymandering might dissipate electoral power or misinformation might create real or perceived limitations to exercising the vote. Perhaps more importantly, the very political options we have—the candidates, parties, and political agendas we choose from—are considerably limited by, even beholden to, wider interests and influences. Structure clearly constrains access, choices, agendas, and actual political decision making and policy, regardless of citizens' desires. Further, those in privileged positions will, by and large, hold the structural and institutional tools to reinforce prevailing power hierarchies.

The role of structure in bolstering power differentials is equally true of other institutional realms. Employees, for instance, are typically bound to procedural manuals, existing technological controls, or the speed of machinery, and they have fewer protections than they've had in the past. Supervisors can invoke (or not invoke) elements of authority and sanctioning like hiring, firing, demoting, and promoting, often with little repercussion. This is particularly true when shielded by legal precedence and financial advantage (that is, laws like corporate personhood protect many in powerful positions in the corporate world and, if they are challenged, money can allow for a great advantage in the courtroom). A similar case can be made for medical access, where power to obtain treatment is conditioned by resources, rules, and social safety nets dictated by government officials, insurance companies, and the pharmaceutical industry. Even medical practitioners are increasingly constrained by structures leveraged by even more influential actors and entities. In these regards, power is vested in the system—or, to be more precise, in how social relations are structured and maintained within institutional and organizational contexts.

That powerful actors have the capacity to create or invoke structure in their own interests while the less powerful are more constrained is an important sociological point, yet it is typically hidden by our everyday understandings of how organizations and institutions operate. Indeed, we tend to see contemporary structures and rules as more or less bureaucratic, rational, and neutral. And, to be sure, they are presented that way. Yet, significant inequalities exist across most institutional domains, including politics. Consider, for instance, who is represented, who has voice, who benefits from policies, and which agendas reach the table.

In one clear example, in recent years, agents of large and powerful financial institutions manipulated the stock market and gambled on high-risk mortgages for the sake of massive personal and institutional financial gains. To prevent more devastating losses to shareholders and the public, these companies were "bailed out" by the federal government, with some bailout money going toward financial bonuses for CEOs. Few were prosecuted for mismanagement, and fewer still were characterized as criminals, to the outrage of an electorate that has seen its social safety nets evaporate, housing values deteriorate, retirement accounts dwindle, reproductive rights attacked, job prospects collapse, and the possibility of universal health care taken off the table. "Power begets power" rings apparent; the less powerful were left paying the bill.

Such a disconnect, I would submit, is due to the fact that we tend not to see large-scale abuses as unjust exercises of power so much as the unfortunate results of an amorphous "bad social system." What we forget—or choose to overlook—is that this "unfortunately bad system" benefits those who constructed and control it in the first place. Equally misguided is a focus on the micro level: equating misconduct with "a few bad apples." That view ascribes abuses of power to individual defect, obfuscating its structural and systemic character. Instead, we must return to the fact that structure bolsters power for some and mitigates it for others.

cultural scaffolding and the legitimation of power

Power relations and the structures that support them, according to classic and more contemporary sociological work by scholars including Antonio Gramsci, Pierre Bourdieu, and L. Richard Delia Fave, are typically buttressed by what I call "cultural scaffolding"—that is, values and belief systems that portray power and its use as reasonable and legitimate. Popular portrayals, in fact, remain largely loyal to neutral assumptions about how power operates, rarely question the legitimacy of those in power or the cultural symbolism they invoke, and often seem unaware of the cultural foundations that reinforce unequal power relations in organizational, institutional, and political life. The sociological focus on cultural scaffolding forces attention toward the ways in which power differentials and the exercise of power itself are legitimated—made to seem reasonable, just, rational, and even natural.

Language and symbolism are important in these regards, especially when it comes to *symbolic vilification*. Symbolic vilification is the process whereby the powerful scapegoat opponents or less powerful actors by deeming them less worthy, problematic, or even dangerous. When this occurs, it is easier to maintain power by creating fear, reify inequality through exclusion, apply punitive sanctions and control policies, or even invoke violence toward subordinated groups, as Erich Goode and Nachman Ben-Yehuda, as well as Joshua Guetzkow, have observed. A second, often simultaneous process entails *symbolic amplification*, which occurs when actors imbue and elevate certain elements of cultural, institutional/organizational, and political life to a place of almost sacred reverence. One might consider broadly constructed cultural values (say, freedom, democracy, and equality) in this light, but also more institutionally and organizationally specific processes like educational choice, religious piety, or "family values."

All actors, of course, can invoke such symbols. Social movements typically do so in an effort to galvanize commitment, participation, and public support, find scholars like David A. Snow and Robert D. Benford. Importantly, though, symbolic amplification is also commonly mobilized in defense of institutional power, practices, and privilege. That is, symbolic amplification can be used in conservative ways that defend the status quo.

Sociologists may seem unique in our emphasis on culture and the dynamics of "legitimation," but political parties and candidates are well aware of the effects. They work incredibly hard to frame issues in a manner consistent with the identities and value systems of their targeted demographic voting groups. This is easily witnessed in, for example, the political use of the terms *democracy* and *freedom* relative to the vilification of immigrants, minorities, and labor unions.

To further clarify, I offer two other brief examples. First, there is American public education, which has witnessed dramatic changes over the last decade. This change has come under the rubric of educational "competition" and "accountability." States and advocates, hoping to garner public support and push through various alternatives (voucher systems, charter schools, etc.) quickly mimicked one another in amplifying these values, while simultaneously blaming teachers, teacher unions, and tenure-based systems for "poorly performing schools." Simultaneous amplification and vilification, in this case, provided the cultural scaffolding to legitimate policy changes—changes that have had greater benefits for already advantaged populations and have led to increasing levels of segregation, as documented by contemporary scholars Gary Orfield and Linda A. Renzulli.

My second example comes from the years I spent examining workplace discrimination. In that research, I did find some examples of "bad apples" in otherwise good environments, yet in the vast majority of cases, employers used otherwise neutral bureaucratic rules and procedures to systematically fire, demote, not promote, and harass minority, female, and aging employees. These employers defended their actions by simultaneously amplifying claims of merit, business interest, and neutrality (often pointing to official bureaucratic rules) while also vilifying victims as unstable, unreliable, and problematic. The use of ostensibly neutral rules and structure by powerful actors was clear, as was the cultural scaffolding that legitimated their discriminatory conduct.

Culture and legitimation are undoubtedly elemental to understanding power within any institutional or organizational context. Cultural values and symbolism are invoked by those in power or vying for power, sometimes to manipulate, sometimes to blur complex issues, and certainly to bolster allegiance and an image of fairness, neutrality, and trustworthiness. Such processes also reduce the chances that less powerful actors, be they in politics or some other institutional domain, will recognize or act upon alternatives, abuses, or the inequalities that often result.

relations of power and challenge

Given structural and cultural advantages, one might simply conclude that the powerful are secure. They may be, to some degree, given the complex conjuncture of structure and culture that privileges the status quo. But sociological luminary Frances Fox Piven reminds us that history reveals important caveats and insights regarding the fundamentally relational nature of power. Power is, after all, ultimately dependent on the perceptions of and compliance by the population at large. Recognizing this, Piven explains, can reveal points where power might be effectively challenged—or at least held in check.

One such opening is found in the fit between official decrees, supposed goals, and the invoking of valued cultural symbols with *actual* policies and practice. Indeed, the alignment of official claims and practice should be a core focal point for sociologists, policymakers, and those on the legal-judicial and activist fronts. Elite vulnerability to challenge may emerge if efforts at vilification do not resonate, cannot be squared with the facts, or meet with some form of backlash or when powerful actors' behaviors are revealed as hypocritical. In these situations, individual and collective action can pose a counterbalance to current power. Individuals, of course, have *always* resisted inequality and power relations in everyday life, be it through direct confrontation, silent resistance, compliance, or the use of more formal channels such as grievance procedures or legal disputes. As I have noted, however, the playing field is quite uneven. By virtue of bureaucratic access, positions, and resources, those in power have both culturally proscribed authority and a better chance to create and implement the rules by which we are all to play. Such advantages confer greater structural and cultural leverage.

Collective action is another important counterweight to standing power. The success of movements often depends on the degree to which the action explicitly challenges (and succeeds at challenging) the structural and cultural bases of power. Certain movements (like the civil rights movement of the 1960s) have been effective by employing tactics of civil disobedience—disruptive tactics that directly challenge institutional and structural dictates, often while making moral claims, in order to bring attention to power imbalances. Most contemporary social movements choose instead to work within existing institutional and cultural structures, though this blunts movements' impact by constraining their actions to those that are not disruptive. Some recent exceptions to this pattern include the Arab Spring, which directly defied political control and authority, and waves of same-sex marriage ceremonies orchestrated by ministers in the United States, despite their illegality at the state level. In each case, structural and cultural underpinnings were directly confronted.

Still, most contemporary social movement activities might be best described as legal and organized consciousness-raising activities. These efforts maybe effective, but likely only to the extent that the message resonates widely enough that power holders are forced to cater to a sizeable voting block. The Occupy Wall Street movement held this potential and certainly altered to some extent the language the powerful used in their appeals to the broader voting public. It is unclear, however, whether the ideas and words of movements—even if adopted into the framing and rhetoric of the powerful—will result in systemic, structural transformations (especially, as in the case of Occupy, as the movement declines in participation and visibility). Effective challenge, whether individual or collective, must confront the structural and cultural foundations that sustain the bases and practices of power.

Grounded in the study of multiple institutional and organizational arenas, sociological insights on power can and should be extended to our understanding of politics. This includes the politics occurring right before our eyes in local and national races and as policies are implemented on the ground, but also *general* conceptions of political power. Just the other day I began imagining similar processes as they must have occurred in ancient Rome. There goes Julius Caesar, I thought, making populist appeals for a fairer distribution of resources so as to galvanize his solitary power. And there, the Roman Senate, comprised of elites, appealing to the preservation of "democratic" governance. Surely the structural, cultural, and relational nature of power about which I have written were as relevant in the face of the inequalities and politics of power in ancient Rome as they are in contemporary China, the United States, and throughout the Middle East.

None of this, of course, is to suggest that there are not differences in the practice of power across historical and contemporary contexts or that there are no divergences between specific power holders or political parties. There certainly are. The extent of true change, however, lies in the ability to transform structure and culture in meaningful ways, and it is difficult to imagine that the source of fundamental transformation will emerge from power itself, vested as it is in established structural and cultural arrangements. Small differences between political actors and parties may be enough for the populace. Or, perhaps unforeseen movements will emerge to challenge, shake, or transform current power relations and the structural-cultural foundations that support them. I am certain of none of this. What I am sure of is that sociology provides the keenest and most in-depth tools through which to see, dissect, and understand how power, including that surrounding politics, operates.

RECOMMENDED READING

Pierre Bourdieu. 1991. *Language and Symbolic Power*, Cambridge, U.K.: Polity Press. In this classic work, Bourdieu captures and explains the essence of culture and language, along with the ways in which they create and solidify societal divides.

L. Richard Delia Fave. 1986. "Toward an Explication of the Legitimation Process," *Social Forces* 65(2):476–500. Provides sociological insight into the dynamics of legitimation as they relate to inequality and the possibilities of challenging power.

Joshua Guetzkow. 2010. "Beyond Deservingness: Congressional Discourse on Poverty, 1964–1996," *Annals of the American Academy of Political and Social Sciences* 629(1):173–197. Presents important and direct analyses of how the linguistic framing of the nature of poverty precedes the construction and enactment of political policy.

Frances Fox Piven. 2008. "Can Power from Below Change the World?" *American Sociological Review* 73(1):1–14. In this presidential address to the American Sociological Association, Piven reminds the reader how and why power is never absolute and offers insight into the leverage less powerful actors might express.

Cecilia Ridgeway and Lynn Smith-Lovin. 1999. "The Gender System and Interaction," *Annual Review of Sociology* 25:191–216. Provides an important overview of power as it relates to status, interaction, and structure relative to gender and inequality.

polling, politics, and the populace according to goren, schuman, and smith

2

KYLE GREEN

E very news-consuming American knows there's always a ballot or an election on the horizon. As stats are shot at us from left and right, it is difficult to go a day without hearing the most recent reports on which candidate has taken the lead, who has gained momentum, and who or what is no longer viable. This leads to two rather important, but rarely asked, questions: who cares and what do these numbers really mean? In this roundtable, we hope to provide a basic understanding of polling, its different forms, how it is used by the candidates, campaigns, and the media—and what insight sociologists can provide.

What is polling and what does it measure?

Howard Schuman: A poll is almost always a series of questions intended to provide information about a large population (one too big to talk to one on one). For example, the total American population, which is now over 300 million people, or you can be interested only in American adults, say, age 18 and over. A poll does this by drawing a relatively small sample from the population, then using probability theory to generalize the sample results to the entire population.

Surveys or polls can be used for practically any issue you wish to ask about, whether it's factual, attitudes, beliefs, values, or anything else you can think to ask people. Most people are familiar with polls that measure opinions about political candidates, including who will win an election, but there's really no limit to the types of topics that a poll or survey can ask about. For example, the federal government uses surveys each month to measure unemployment. So when you hear a figure like "There's 8.2% unemployment over the past month," it's based on a sample. It's a fairly large sample, but still, it's a very small part of the total population of the U.S. labor force, so the government uses a survey to determine and report on unemployment every month. And much else that appears in government reports is based on samples of either the total population or some part of the population.

The questions themselves matter. And it turns out that writing questions is a lot more complex than most people realize. Answers can be affected by the form of the question—that is, whether it is open-ended or closed. The words also matter. For example, there's no real difference between "forbidding" smoking and "not allowing" smoking in, say, a classroom, but many Americans give different answers to the question depending on whether you say "Should smoking be forbidden?" or "Should it not be allowed?" So, wording can make a huge difference. A third factor that affects answers is the context of the question. This includes the order of the questions—what questions came before—and also if there's an interviewer, the race and sex of the interviewer often affect the answers, particularly if the questions deal with race or gender.

Let me add that anyone who watches television, reads newspapers, or looks at the Internet will see lots of polls. They've increased enormously since first developed (usually traced to the mid-1930s), so today polls proliferate on all subjects and very much on any political issue, and of course on the Republican nominating process and so forth. They've really become overwhelming, and it's important to try to distinguish good from bad surveys.

What are the uses and limitations of polling?

Paul Goren: Well, one big limitation is that a slight change or slight alteration of a particular phrase or the inclusion or exclusion of a particular adjective can change poll responses a lot. For instance, you ask the question, "Should we spend more, spend less, or spend about the same on Social Security?" you might find 53% of the public says, "Let's spend more on Social Security." And then if we run the survey using the following wording: "Should we spend more, spend less, or spend about the same on protecting Social Security?" just by adding the one word *protecting*, support for spending on Social Security might move 15% in the liberal direction. And so if you have a poll that's run by the National Rifle Association or the Sierra Club—any group with an obvious stake in the outcome of the polls—you can probably discount it. Even legitimate polling organizations like Gallup and NBC/Wall Street Journal, you have to look at that question wording very carefully because just a slight change, a slight tweak can lead to substantially different results. If 53% say we should spend more, that's a majority; if it's 68%, that's a supermajority, and that suggests you've got more of the public with you, when it may just be the reaction to that one word, the idiosyncrasy of that one question. So the question wording is one thing you should pay close attention to.

The trick there is . . . can you consult multiple polls? Again, an example I always use with my students, the problem with relying on results from a single survey question is "On your final exam, how many of you would like to have one multiple-choice question?" Show of hands? Nobody puts their hand up. "How about a hundred multiple-choice questions?" All the hands go up. Because that one question could be the one that they don't know, and they could get wiped out to zero. Same with public opinion: Why would you try to measure the public's perceptions on an issue using one question? You wouldn't use a hundred, but maybe two, three, four, or five polls that ask about the same thing.

So, if politicians are smart, they'll look at poll results, but not just from one survey, particularly one survey or one question that seems to confirm their preexisting bias; they should look at several polls with several questions. But, you know, they're politicians, they were elected to do x, y, and z, they want to see the public is with them, and so they may resist that temptation to try to be open-minded and inclusive in their assessment of polling data!

Schuman: One problem is that polls tend to construct what's happening. That is, people hear that some issue is very prominent at the moment, and that then influences what they think is the important issue of the day.

There is certainly a tendency to dismiss polls, but usually they get dismissed by people who don't like the results. And the same person who says, "Oh, I don't believe polls; how can you do that with so few people?" and so forth is apt to defend a poll if it goes in a direction they favor! So, I don't take critics too seriously—of course many polls are trivial and many polls are badly done, but the criticisms are usually based on whether the results agree or disagree with what you think.

That being said, there are many problems that come up when doing a survey, and these apply both to sampling and to question-asking. In the case of sampling, not everyone is willing to answer questions or can even be located. The proportion of people who take part in the survey is called the "response rate" for the survey, and response rates have been dropping in recent years. Rates were around 80% in the 1950s and are now under 10%, though much higher for government surveys, especially those where participation is legally required. There are ways to compensate for the bias that nonresponse introduces, but the compensation cannot be perfect and it lends more uncertainty into almost all poll reports these days.

Also, to the extent that the questions asked are not good measures of what you intend to measure, results are less valid. A big problem in constructing questions is that every big issue has many different aspects. . . . So, although some people are against all abortions and some people would leave all abortions up to a woman's choice, most respondents to a survey will give different answers depending on how you specify the reasons for the abortion and the time it occurs, so really, it doesn't make sense to ask a general question about abortion ("Do you favor or oppose?" or whatever). Questions are almost always better if they are more specific. . . . And that's true of almost any other issue, whether it's gun control, Iran's development of nuclear weapons, Obama's health reform legislation—in all these cases, the question has to be useful to begin to deal with the specificities.

Can you provide a brief contextualization of the role polling plays in the political process?

Tom Smith: Polling is used for many different purposes in the political process, including, but not limited to, so-called horse-race questions about the candidate one intends to vote for, the likelihood of voting, familiarity with candidates and issues, message testing, and assessment of campaign ads. The polls may be directed to the whole electorate, likely voters, members of one political party only, or some special target group (e.g., Hispanics or first-time voters). They range from high-quality, well-designed surveys down to virtual junk based on tiny samples, biased questions, and other shoddy parts.

When done well, polls provide valuable information to a campaign and can greatly improve a candidate's chances of success in an election. But polls are often poorly done. First, campaigns and their consultants may lack the technical competency to design and carry out surveys properly or lack the resources to do scientifically credible work. Second, campaigns often need very up-to-date information (e.g., after a debate or the emergence of some damaging news) and there may be neither the time nor resources to measure the impact of the breaking development.

Goren: Polls have been part of the political system of campaigns and elections for a very long time. There's some good archival research that shows that presidents Kennedy, Johnson, and Nixon paid a lot of attention to internal polls to get an idea of what kind of policies they could pursue, how far they could go, and things of that nature. Polling has informed, or at least served as a guideline, for presidential decision making for a long time. But over the past couple of decades, it's really taken off. There is now polling data all over the place.

One way it matters is that politicians can get a very good sense of where the public stands on any particular issue at any particular point in time. Whether politicians choose to pay much attention or much heed to those polling data is a different story. Sometimes the polls suggest politicians should not pursue a given policy, and politicians, by virtue of, say, a big win on Election Day, might think they have a mandate from the voters and try to move in a direction even though the public opinion polls suggest it might get them in some trouble. One example of politicians taking such a risk would be when the Republicans had their big win in the midterm election of 2010. Historically large, but not unprecedented, it was a very, very big win for the Republicans. And a lot of Republicans in the House took that as evidence that the voters wanted them to move in a very conservative direction on entitlement programs— take Medicare and change it from an entitlement program to a voucher program. . . . But when the polling results started coming back, they started getting a lot of heat for that.

The voting process is often placed under the domain of political scientists. How does a sociological approach differ from, or supplement, that found in political science?

Smith: While elections and campaigns may formally be under the domain of political science rather than sociology, sociologists can play an important role in the use of political polls. The topic of public opinion falls as much under sociology as under political science. Sociologists are particularly adept at understanding social change and how short- and long-term trends may be reshaping both society as a whole and the body politic in particular. Sociologists in particular have a good grasp of cohort differences and how these may be changing the political climate. They are also well tuned to understanding subgroup dynamics and the role of different groups such as ethnicities, genders, and classes in the political process. Political scientists sometimes have a narrower political focus, while sociologists are more likely to have a more holistic understanding of voters.

Schuman: I can give you an example from my own research, which is quite different from political polling. I've been doing, for the last few years, studies of what is called "collective memory"—that is, how people think about important national and world events from the past, such as the 9/11 terrorist attack, the invasion of Iraq, the assassination back in the '60s of President Kennedy, and even going back to how they think about World War II. I've had a guiding hypothesis—shared by someone working with me, Amy Corning—that most people remember best those events that occurred when they were growing up (roughly ages 10 to 30). That is, if you ask them "What are the important events over, say, the last 100 years?" most people will give an event that occurred when they were, themselves, adolescents or in very early adulthood, no matter what their present age is. We've investigated this not only with American data but with data from half a dozen other countries (Germany, Japan, Russia, Israel, Lithuania, and Pakistan), and we did this because we believed the hypothesis to be quite general, not just about people in the United States. So that's an example of something that has nothing to do with predicting who's going to win an election, but it's cross-national and it deals with a kind of fundamental hypothesis about human beings—it's just one example of what sociologists can do with polling and survey data.

Goren: By definition, political scientists care about the subject, right? Otherwise, why would you get a PhD in political science and teach about it? So, people in my particular discipline are deeply informed, deeply knowledgeable about all aspects of politics (what liberalism and conservatism mean, what's in the Affordable Care Act, things of that nature). And then when you come across poll results that find that what the public knows is just shockingly low or abysmally low, people are just blown away! And so political scientists—not all of us, but a lot of people in my discipline—when they see that only 20% of the public knows that John Roberts is the Chief Justice of the Supreme Court, they say, "Oh my gosh! That's why democracy is in such a sorry state!" . . . But despite my lack of knowledge, I still might be a very reasonable voter . . . John Roberts might be the utility infielder who played for the Minnesota Twins seven years ago for all I know, but . . . even though I know very little about politics, it still might be a very reasonable choice that I would make on Election Day. And so political scientists [might be] so single-mindedly focused on political matters they miss the big picture! What I've noticed, at least among the folks in sociology, they tend to look at polls not simply in the context of politics but some aspects of politics and society more broadly.

PARTICIPANT PROFILES

Paul Goren is a political scientist at the University of Minnesota. He studies public opinion, voting behavior, and applied statistics and econometrics.

Howard Schuman is a professor emeritus of sociology at the University of Michigan. He is the author of *Method and Meanings in Polls and Surveys* (2011, Harvard University Press).

Tom Smith is a senior fellow at and the director of the Center for the Study of Politics and Society at the University of Chicago's NORC. He is the editor of *Public Opinion Quarterly*.

social fact: those who can, vote?

DEBORAH CARR

n the weeks leading up to the November 2012 presidential election, college campuses teemed with young volunteers urging their classmates to register online to vote. Miles away from the Ivy towers and frat rows, dedicated volunteers (typically for the Democratic party) clutched their clipboards outside bodegas, pounded the pavement at inner-city block parties, and approached tired commuters at bus and subway stations, asking everyone they could whether they'd like to register to vote.

These efforts were well intended; low voter turnout rates among young Americans, the poor, and ethnic minorities have the potential to profoundly affect election results—especially given the tendency of each of these subgroups to favor Democrats in national elections. The proportion of 18- to 24-year-olds who voted in the 2008 presidential election is estimated to have reached 51%. Although that marked the third highest turnout rate among young people since the voting age was lowered to 18 in 1971, the figure still lags far behind the 70% turnout rate evidenced among voters in their 50s and older. Some observers estimate this age gap means that 25 to 30 million youth votes are "missing" and up for grabs.

Why aren't young people—as well as ethnic minorities and the economically disadvantaged—turning out on Election Day? One widely accepted answer is access; those who don't register can't vote. There is some truth to this explanation. The Current Population Survey, a random sample survey of Americans, asks participants whether they were registered to vote and whether they *did* vote in the most recent election prior to the interview. Some of the data capturing 2008 voting behavior are plotted in three graphics on pp. 35–36. Just half of 18- to 20-year-olds and 56% of 21- to 24-year-olds say they registered to vote in the 2008 presidential election, compared to 75% of persons age 65 and older. Even wider disparities are evidenced by ethnicity: while three quarters of whites and blacks say they were registered to vote in the 2008 election, just 37% of Asian and Latino respondents had registered. Further, the educational gradient in voter registration is remarkably steep: fewer than one third of persons with an 8th grade education registered, but the proportion climbed to 43% among high school dropouts, 60% among high school graduates, 72% among those with some college, and 77% for college graduates.

FIGURE 3.1 **Likelihood of Registering & Voting in the 2008 Presidential Election by Age**

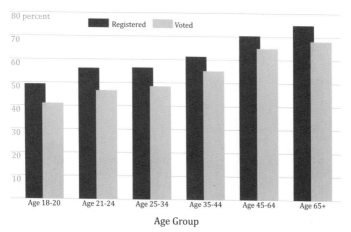

Source: U.S. Census Bureau, *Voting and Registration in the Election of November 2010*, Current Population Reports, P20-562, 2010.
http://www.census.gov/compendia/statab/2012/tables/12s0399.pdf, accessed October 20, 2012.

FIGURE 3.2 **Likelihood of Registering & Voting in the 2008 Presidential Election by Level of Education**

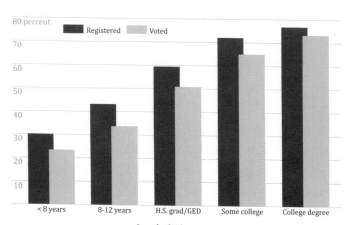

Source: U.S. Census Bureau, *Voting and Registration in the Election of November 2010*, Current Population Reports, P20-562, 2010.
http://www.census.gov/compendia/statab/2012/tables/12s0399.pdf, accessed October 20, 2012.

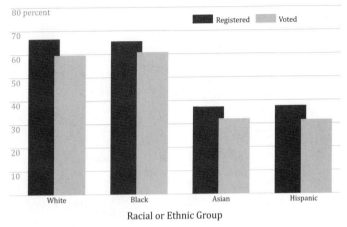

FIGURE 3.3 **Likelihood of Registering & Voting in the 2008 Presidential Election by Race or Ethnic Group**

Racial or Ethnic Group

Source: U.S. Census Bureau, *Voting and Registration in the Election of November 2010*, Current Population Reports, P20-562, 2010. http://www.census.gov/compendia/statab/2012/tables/12s0399.pdf, accessed October 20, 2012.

These wide disparities in voter registration are exacerbated by the fact that many who register to vote do not ultimately turn out to the polls. The proportion of registered voters who fail to vote is steepest among young people, the poorly educated, Asians, and Hispanics. For example, 68% of persons age 65 and older said they voted in the 2008 election—that's more than 90% of those who said they had been registered. By contrast, 41% of persons ages 18 to 20 voted, for 84% of those who had registered. The gaps are steeper by educational attainment: nearly all college graduates who were registered ultimately voted, yet just three quarters of those with an 8th grade education could say the same.

The question remains: Why are some Americans less likely to register and, ultimately, to vote? Experts attribute these patterns to a range of factors including apathy, disillusionment, a lack of civics education, the belief that neither candidate represents one's interests, and high exposure to television ads that smear the candidates' reputations. Yet some political observers anticipate an increase in young and economically disadvantaged voters. After all, the issues considered most important in today's elections are joblessness and the flailing economy—concerns that may well trigger a strong turnout among those facing the bleakest economic and career prospects.

movements + elections = democracy

STEVEN BUECHLER

here have been unusually high levels of movement mobilization since the last presidential election. Within a year of Obama's landmark 2008 victory, an economic crisis and political backlash sparked a Tea Party movement that dramatically affected the 2010 midterm elections and pulled the entire Republican Party further to the right. The polarizing effect of movements on parties and the tension between ideological purity and securing moderate voters were much in evidence throughout the Republican primaries and continued to haunt the Romney/Ryan campaign in particular.

The economic crisis, of course, also sparked another mobilization whose occupation of Zuccotti Park in New York City occurred just under two years ago. Part protest, part demonstration, part carnival, part counterculture, the Occupy Wall Street movement featured an almost impossibly diverse range of issues and constituencies (a prominent poster at Occupy Minneapolis: "I'll believe corporations are people when Texas executes one"). But at its heart, Occupy challenged the neoliberal narrative, refocused attention on economic inequality, provided a populist counternarrative, and reinvigorated and cultivated progressive voices.

Such activism is a potent reminder that politics in a democracy involves more than just elections. And while the impacts of movements and the outcomes of elections are difficult to predict (and in some cases, assess), sociology provides lasting utility in explaining the social forces that shape movements and their political legacies.

toward a social movement society

Over the last two centuries, social movements have moved from the margins of society to a much more centralized and persistent presence. While the institutionalization of a particular movement can spell the end of effective activism, the *broader* institutionalization of movements as a form of contentious politics (whereby ordinary people engage in collective action to pursue their interests) has significantly changed our contemporary societal landscape.

The increasing prominence of social movements in societal dynamics is a theme in at least two recent theoretical traditions in sociology. First, consider how the *resource mobilization* approach uses economic imagery to capture the multiple levels in which movements are embedded.

In this paradigm, movements are defined as preferences for change in a population, but such preferences must be converted into action through social movement organizations. These organizations are, in turn, embedded in larger social movement industries comprised of all the social movement organizations acting on similar preferences for change.

And, above social movement industries, there is an even larger unit of analysis: all the social movement industries in a society comprise the *social movement sector* of that society. With the concept of a social movement sector, resource mobilization theory asserts that movements have become a permanent, institutionalized presence, coexisting alongside other well-entrenched social institutions. As John D. McCarthy and Mayer N. Zald have put it, particular movements may wax and wane, but the social movement sector and its rich repertoire of contention is now a defining feature of late modern society.

In a similar vein, Sidney Tarrow has suggested we are entering a new historical period he calls a *movement society*. This is the culmination of a two-hundred-year process. For Tarrow, movements originated in the context of nation-state consolidation. Early challenges to the gathering of state power, however, often had a local, fleeting, temporary character. In the modern era, Tarrow says, "the world may be moving from a logic of alternation between periods of movement and periods of quiescence into a permanent movement society."

In this society, movements deploy a repertoire of contention diffused through global communication networks to create virtually simultaneous and synchronized protest actions. On a more ominous note, Tarrow implies that globalization may leave transnational movements less subject to state control and that their repertoire and tactics may become more violent. While this assertion is open to dispute, Tarrow's underlying premise is clear: Social movements are here to stay.

social movements and democratization

The politics of social movements vary widely. Michael Schwartz was one of my mentors in graduate school who claimed that although not all social movements are progressive, all progressive change comes from social movements. There's an appealing logic here. Why would elites ever accept cuts to their power, privilege, or property unless effectively challenged from below? Moreover, there is abundant evidence that when movements succeed, it's less by changing attitudes than by raising the costs of "business as usual" to a point where elites are compelled to make concessions they otherwise would not.

Our richest historical analyses broadly support this logic while revealing more subtle nuances in the relationships between social movements and democratization. More than anyone else, sociologist Charles Tilly is an insightful guide through this terrain; he identified at least five reciprocal connections between democracy and social movements.

First, Tilly defined democratic regimes as involving relatively broad and equal citizenship, binding consultation between citizens and governments, and protection of citizens from arbitrary actions by government agents. He regards democracy not as a structure or even a set of institutions but as a *process*. And this process can move in either direction: democratization or de-democratization. While the broad trend of the last two centuries has been toward democratization, there is nothing inevitable or irreversible about it.

Second, Tilly clarified that, whether you look historically or cross-nationally, you find that the more democratic the government, the greater the range and variety of social movement contention. Thus, with little or no democratization, you get no social movements. With incipient democratization, you get limited protest, but not full-fledged movements. With further democratization, you find actual movements in limited arenas, but they don't easily spill out into other arenas. And finally, with extensive democratization, there is a widespread availability of movement repertoires that readily diffuse across different arenas and constituencies.

Third, there are some processes, Tilly observes, that act in the background to promote both democratization and social movements. Any demographic, technological, or other social change that increases social networks, equalizes access to resources, insulates public politics from existing inequalities, or proliferates trust networks will facilitate both democratization and social movements.

Fourth, democratization independently promotes social movements by broadening and equalizing rights, increasing binding consultation, and expanding citizen protections. As noted earlier, however, de-democratization can just as easily reverse these gains.

Finally, Tilly finds social movements independently promote democracy when enough democracy already exists to allow them to mobilize popular support, broaden the range of participants, equalize various participants, and at least partially neutralize the effect of categorical inequalities on public politics.

In Tilly's big picture, then, social movements and democratization reinforce each other in a virtuous cycle. This broad generalization is a good working tool, so long as we remember there's lots of room for reversals, anomalies, and exceptions to the dominant pattern.

social movements and electoral contention

Now we can drop down several levels of abstraction to examine the more specific dynamics of political protest and electoral politics. This is the terrain of Frances Fox Piven, whose work reveals the logic of *disruptive power* as a movement strategy to alter electoral outcomes.

Here's Piven's argument: In everyday social life, we are embedded in multiple social networks of cooperation. When we deliberately withhold cooperation, the resulting disruption of those networks creates power for otherwise powerless people. Strikes, boycotts, occupations, and civil disobedience are all examples of such disruptive power in action.

Disruption thus derives its leverage from the breakdown of institutionally regulated cooperation. It occurs when movements violate rules, demand nonnegotiable concessions, or use unconventional or illegal forms of collective action to their advantage.

Piven echoes my mentor Schwartz in saying that most major reforms in American history have been won through the mobilization of disruptive power. At the same time, she acknowledges that using such power is a form of high-risk activism whose occasional gains are often reversed when the disruption inevitably fades away.

But what about elections? In Piven's view, electoral politics can play an important role in policy formation, but normally electoral politics are dominated by elite interests and inevitably lead to pro-elite policies. This only changes when people engage in disruptive politics outside the electoral arena. Then disruptive power fractures conventional electoral coalitions and voting blocs within parties. It spurs the defection of some voters and necessitates attempts to gain new ones. In these ways, disruptive power moves electoral politics out of its routine, elite-dominated mold and makes it more responsive to ordinary people and long-neglected needs.

Mass defiance can thus promote progressive policy in two ways. The direct path is when the defiance is substantial enough to constrain elites and their choices, regardless of the electoral cycle. The indirect path is when mass defiance changes the logic of electoral politics, fractures old voting blocs, creates new alliances, and thereby creates opportunities for progressive policy formation.

To summarize, while Tilly paints a historical overview of the intertwined nature of movements and democracy, Piven offers a more specific analysis of how disruptive power can alter the logic of electoral politics and foster more democratic outcomes. But she also sounds a cautionary note about how easily de-democratization can reverse progress in the absence of sustained disruption.

A final piece of scholarship further enriches our understanding of these issues. In a forthcoming book chapter, Doug McAdam and Sidney Tarrow take their own look at the role of movements in electoral contention. Their work bridges Tilly's broad generalities and Piven's detailed analysis, starting with the premise that social movements and institutional politics mutually constitute each other in at least five ways.

One of the more familiar links occurs when movements make a tactical decision to devote their often-scarce resources to sponsoring parties and candidates in electoral campaigns—the *electoral option.* Although this may be more effective in systems based on proportional representation than in the winner-take-all districts found in the United States, there has been no shortage of third-party movements in this country. Their success on the national level has been limited, but our decentralized system has permitted more influence for these groups at the state, county, and municipal levels.

A related process is *proactive electoral mobilization.* Here, electoral campaigns stimulate renewed movement mobilization when people perceive an upcoming election as providing either a threat or an opportunity in relation to their interests. This impulse may lead back to the electoral option or it may lead to a more sustained mobilization that persists beyond the cyclical dynamics of electoral campaigns.

While proactive electoral mobilization begins before an election, *reactive electoral mobilization* responds to a disputed election with escalating protest. This is more likely in less democratic states, and examples range from Serbia and Zimbabwe to the Philippines and Central Asia. Even the United States, however, saw temporarily heightened protest in response to the highly contested presidential election of 2000 and its dubious resolution by the Supreme Court.

A fourth linkage involves how movements can induce *party polarization*. The stronger the movement, the more candidates feel compelled to appeal to their base, thereby reinforcing this polarizing effect. This process highlights the tension between the centrist, coalitional logic of elections and the uncompromising, purist ideologies of movements. Parties may be both the beneficiaries and the victims of this polarization as electoral rhythms and governing challenges play themselves out.

A final, and much broader process concerns the links between *electoral regimes* lasting decades and the corresponding fates of entire families of movements. In the twentieth century, there were three broad electoral regimes involving Republican domination from 1900 to 1932, Democratic domination from 1932 to 1968, and Republican domination once again from 1968 to 2008. In each period, the dominant party significantly influenced the mobilization opportunities of various movements.

This last process is especially significant because of its historical sweep and its counterintuitive logic. Common sense might be tempted to say that whichever party is in power will provoke movement challenges from opposing forces, but McAdam and Tarrow claim quite the opposite: "Progressive left movements can be expected to flourish during periods of liberal institutional politics, while the right should be ascendant when conservatives hold institutional power." Hence, the progressive movements of the 1930s and 1960s thrived under Democratic dominance, while more conservative movements have proliferated during the more recent decades of Republican dominance.

———

Election season has a way of reducing democracy to little more than politicians, polls, and pundits. The scholarship reviewed here reminds us that electoral politics unfold in a much broader sociohistorical context. A closer look at that context reveals some surprisingly strong links among social movements, progressive politics, electoral dynamics, and the conflicting forces that enhance or diminish democracy.

For example, Piven's approach illuminates how movements like the Tea Party and Occupy Wall Street can shake electoral politics out of their routine, institutional, and pro-elite patterns. Tilly's understanding of democracy as a two-way process highlights the de-democratizing tendencies currently in play, including the Citizens United decision by the Supreme Court, the resulting rise of superPACs, and various campaigns to restrict or suppress voting rights (to name a few). And, finally, McAdam and Tarrow underscore the potential significance of *this* particular election and its potential to extend or interrupt what they characterize as a forty-year, Republican-dominated electoral regime with fateful consequences for social movement mobilization.

Long after the politicians and pundits have exhausted themselves (and us) and the polls have been proven "wrong," such sociological insights will endure as more useful tools for understanding the myriad links among movements, elections, and democracy.

RECOMMENDED READING

Doug McAdam and Sidney Tarrow. 2012. "Social Movements and Elections: Toward a Broader Understanding of the Context of Contention," in *The Changing Dynamics of Contention,* edited by Jacquelien van Stekelenburg, Conny Roggeband, and Bert Klandermans. Minneapolis: University of Minnesota Press.

John D. McCarthy and Mayer N. Zald. 1977. "Resources Mobilization and Social Movements: A Partial Theory," *American Journal of Sociology* 82:1212–1241.

Frances Fox Piven. 2006. *Challenging Authority: How Ordinary People Change America*, Lanham, MD: Rowman & Littlefield.

Sidney Tarrow. 1994. *Power in Movement: Social Movements, Collective Action, and Politics*, New York: Cambridge University Press.

Charles Tilly and Lesley J. Wood. 2013. *Social Movements: 1786–2012* (3rd edition), Boulder, CO: Paradigm.

5

the obama era, the 2012 election, and systemic racism

JOE R. FEAGIN

We are not a fully democratic country. We never have been and now are moving only very slowly in that direction. To understand the 2012 election and key political events in the Obama era, we must look at the larger societal context—at institutional fundamentals. *Systemic racism* is central in that institutional context, and especially in our political system.

Our political institutions were built by elite white male founders (40% of the participants at the U.S. constitutional convention being slaveholders and many of the rest profiting off the slavery system). These men and their descendants built political institutions to protect their racial and class interests, and many were undemocratic or antidemocratic: a Constitution aggressively designed to protect enslaved property; a Senate representing land areas and powerful whites far more than ordinary people; an unelected Supreme Court of elite whites trumping acts of Congress; and an elite white male president chosen by an undemocratic Electoral College. There are too many undemocratic capitalistic institutions to list, all also made and maintained mostly by elite white men substantially to protect their political-economic interests.

Even today, the United States is substantially run by an elite oligarchy of white males. The 112th Congress was overwhelmingly white and male. The Senate was 96% white and 81% white men. The House was 83% white and 72% white men. With only two exceptions (Nancy Pelosi and Barack Obama), the top spots in Congress and the White House have always been held by elite white men. And today, elite white men make up fully 93% of the CEOs of Fortune 500 companies. Regardless of the 2012 election, a small oligarchy of white men still firmly controls America's major political-economic institutions.

That is our current context. Because of our elite-run institutions, the 2012 election wasn't democratic in operation or structure: voters got to vote for white-male-elite- chosen, well-off candidates—choosing between a prototypical rich white man and a black man vetted by and financially indebted to elite whites. Whoever won, a small oligarchy of white men would still firmly control our major political-economic institutions.

Astoundingly, the "founders" and their powerful descendants are still rarely called out as *elite white men* and researched systematically as such by social scientists.

racially polarized electorates

Until the 1960s *almost all* American voters were white. The end of Jim Crow brought a significant increase in voters of color and their important electoral organizations. Since the 1970s, the Democratic Party has been much more racially diverse than the Republican Party, with many liberal leaders and with diverse activists and voters from all racial groups. In contrast, the Republican Party has become in effect the "white party" of the United States in terms of overwhelmingly white leaders, activists, membership, and party positions favoring white interests. Over recent decades, substantial growth in and among voters of color has, in fact, gradually changed U.S. politics. However, as Sean Theriault and other political analysts have shown, the racial and political polarization of major parties in Congress has stemmed from party caucuses becoming less *politically* diverse, as white southern Democrats have been replaced by numerous white Republicans and some Democrats of color, and white northern Republicans have become significantly more conservative.

This growth of two substantially different electorates is a clear sign of contemporary systemic racism. One electorate is very diverse with lots of voters of color—who turn out best for presidential elections and tend to vote for typically more liberal Democratic candidates. The other is mostly made up of white voters with better turnout rates, especially for nonpresidential elections, and tends to vote for conservative Republican candidates. According to the analyses of social commentator Bill Bishop, in the 2008 election, about *half* of all presidential votes were in politically and racially polarized counties in which either Obama or McCain won by at least 20%. The percentage of voters in these "landslide" counties has doubled since 1976, and is related to persistent and substantial residential segregation. Counties in which McCain won with a landslide margin were overwhelmingly white. In Obama's landslide counties, black and Latino residents averaged 43% of the voting age population.

In numerous recent local, state, and national elections, voters of color have increasingly been key. A majority have typically shown opposition to white-oriented Republican candidates and party positions. They typically support large-scale government action aimed at socioeconomic opportunities and upward mobility, such as major education and jobs programs that can help all Americans to achieve the "American dream."

In the 2008 election, a substantial majority (55%) of whites opted for McCain (including 59% of white men). So, Obama was elected in large part because of his overwhelming majority among voters of color. Exit polls showed the latter cast ballots for him in large majorities: 95% of blacks, 67% of Latinos, 62% of Asian Americans, and about 70% of Native Americans. If only white voters had been able to decide the presidential race in pivotal states—such as Florida, Ohio, and Virginia—McCain would have won those states and the general election in a landslide.

a political "outsider within"

Barack Obama is the first person of color to ever gain entry into the highest inner sanctum of the U.S. political elite. In our political system, President Obama has been a classical "outsider within"—a designation that comes with major political disadvantages. For example, numerous liberal analysts have called on him to act like previous presidents who aggressively sought liberal policies, such as Franklin Roosevelt did with 1930s social welfare, New Deal programs across the country. Yet Roosevelt was a consummate white insider with stellar elite connections. In his political and governing efforts, Obama has had to depend, in many ways, on the vacillating sponsorship of white men in the moderate segment of the elite for help in gaining political advances. Often, he hasn't had nearly the economic, political, or social capital needed to take aggressive action on key public policies that a full-fledged member of the white elite would likely have.

In recent years, hundreds of thousands of racist attacks were made on Obama's candidacy and presidency by white conservatives, including those supporting Republican candidates. He regularly faced intensive racist framing that insisted upon, and reinforced, his outsider status in the minds of white conservatives. For example, many Tea Party activists, almost all white, place great emphasis on racial and identity issues—such as where Obama was born and his alleged African-ness. Throughout his political years, vicious imagery had been applied to Obama and his family by both powerful and ordinary whites. In just one example of thousands, according to numerous press reports, in February 2012, a white chief federal district judge used an official courthouse address to e-mail acquaintances a "joke" suggesting that Obama's mixed ancestry might stem from his mother's carousing at a party, and that she might even have had sex with a dog—somehow linking white-black interracial sex to possible sexual bestiality. Such mongrelizing imagery for black Americans is familiar—it's old, white, racist framing, and its extensive use even today signals a still systemic racism.

Even under such attacks, fears about the racial framing of potential white supporters kept Obama's team from speaking substantially about U.S. racism. In the 2008 campaign, only once did his camp explicitly call out racism, and that was because media attacks on Obama's distinguished black pastor, Dr. Jeremiah Wright, forced their hand. Sensitive to views of elite and other white backers, White House officials and campaign advisers later urged President Obama to continue with a pragmatic, moderate political orientation that didn't deal openly with racism (thus appealing to white independents and moderate Democrats). As I write in the fall of 2012, they haven't pressed for any major new antidiscrimination laws or major new economic stimulus programs to create jobs for ordinary Americans, especially Americans of color who still face Depression-level unemployment. Recent comments by David Axelrod, Obama's senior political adviser, have signaled this pro-white strategy. Asked on a May 2011 (MSNBC) *Meet the Press* episode if racism was involved in hostile "birther" attacks, an unusually hesitant Axelrod said, "I have not had that discussion with [Obama], and frankly I'm not going to entertain that question. I don't think that's a worthy question because, in that sense. . . . I don't think it's,

I don't think it's, I don't think—but I don't think, I don't think we . . . I think a lot of Americans were offended by it. Of all stripes." Axelrod's evasion was just another glimpse of the impact of white racial framing and other systemic racism on contemporary U.S. politics.

Obama clearly has progressive policy impulses, but has often been blocked or restricted by the conservative wing of the white elite operating through Republicans in Congress. As he reveals in his books, he is well aware of the racial hostility he and other Americans of color face, but he has accomplished a great deal in spite of sustained opposition, albeit frequently under the radar. For example, he worked with his Department of Justice to focus on doggedly enforcing civil rights laws, including hiring many more lawyers experienced in rights litigation. His administration submitted a human rights report under the United Nations Human Rights Council's review process. As noted well by researcher Robert Watson and reported by investigative journalists like Will Moredock, among others, Obama has worked to expand funding of black colleges; pass hate crimes and health-care legislation; enforce equal pay for women; end the military's "Don't Ask, Don't Tell" policy; end federal defense of DOMA (Defense of Marriage Act); remove the stem-cell research ban; provide new funding for child health; expand student and small business loans; and nominate the first Latina

Supreme Court justice. By means of a cautious and pragmatic progressive approach, and usually with support from the moderate wing of the elite, Obama has been able to achieve certain socially liberal political goals.

2010 republican electoral surge

That pragmatic-liberal, sometimes rights-related action and the fact that Obama is black account for much of the white backlash against him. In the 2010 elections, the portion of white voters opting for Republican House candidates increased, setting a record at 60%. Just 37% of whites chose Democratic candidates. The Democratic Party lost the House and some Senate seats. According to detailed reports by Ronald Brownstein and other reporters at the *National Journal,* in July 2012 national polls revealed that Obama was supported by only 28% of noncollege white men and 37 to 40% of college-educated white men, down from 39 and 42%, respectively, in 2008. His percentage among noncollege white women was 37 to 40% and among college-educated white women, 49 to 52% (both figures also down a little from 2008). The same polls showed Obama again getting the overwhelming majority of 69 to 76% of voters of color.

So it is that many political observers viewed the 2012 election as a battle between a still heavily white, conservative electorate and a moderate-to-liberal electorate substantially composed of voters of color.

Various 2008–2011 exit polls, national surveys, and media commentaries indicate that a great many whites view the Democratic Party and its policymaking as much too oriented to interests of voters of color, especially African Americans. That is probably why the "lazy welfare recipient" imagery in Mitt Romney ads, in regard to Obama's recent decision about making work requirements more flexible for a welfare program, has worked well among whites. Increasingly, a great many whites seem to fear the loss of their great socioeconomic privileges and political power to Americans of color. It's no wonder so many have joined very conservative political groups like the Tea Party.

voters of color and obama's campaign strategy

Since the major Democratic Party losses in the 2010 elections, Obama and his campaign staff had to be aware of these results' racial and political implications. The Obama team brought in veteran Katherine Archuleta as its political director for 2012—the first-ever Latina. The campaign seemed to know well their 2008 victory came from constructing the strongest multiracial coalition and presidential campaign in U.S. history, and they needed to work to rebuild it.

Obama got about 80% of all voters of color in 2008. Their 26% of all voters has increased since, significantly in some states and especially among Latinos. Writing in a July 9, 2012, issue of the *New Republic*, political and demographic analysts Ruy Teixeira and William Frey offered important data on the shifts in the electorate over recent decades. That 2008 figure marked a major change from the 1992 election, in which 88% of voters had been white, and some 53% noncollege whites; by 2008 the comparable figures were substantially lower at 74% and 39%, respectively. Significantly, the percentage of eligible voters of color among all voters has increased nationally by 3% since 2008. The share for working-class whites has decreased by that amount, and college-educated whites' share of the votes has stayed about the same. Increases in voters of color are particularly dramatic in "swing" states: in Nevada, the share has increased by 9%; in Colorado 3%; in North Carolina and Florida, about 4%. In contrast, the shares of noncollege white eligible voters have decreased in all four states.

One important strategy for the Obama campaign included getting these eligible voters registered and enthusiastic about voting. Obama's sometimes low-key approach on certain issues of great concern to them has periodically lessened enthusiasm and turnout, even as aggressive, mostly white-run,

Republican attempts to block voters of color have been found in numerous states. In Pennsylvania, the Republican leader in the state House asserted plainly that his state's new voter identification law would "allow Governor Romney to win ... Pennsylvania." New York University's Brennan Center's president Michael Waldman summarized their report naming nineteen states that "rushed through new laws that cut back on voting rights [making it] far harder for millions of eligible citizens to vote" and noting that, luckily, the "Justice Department, courts, and voters have blocked or blunted many of these laws." Yet not all. Significant numbers of voters of color were still likely screened out of the 2012 election.

forever a white oligarchy?

Extensive data show our political and economic systems remain extraordinarily oligarchical. A very small group of wealthy, overwhelmingly white Americans—the famous "one percent"—have far greater political power and control than ordinary Americans of all backgrounds. Substantial research by Jeffrey Winters and Benjamin Page, among others, has shown they effectively control all major public elections and much important policymaking.

One collaborative study by the Public Campaign, the Fannie Lou Hamer Project, and the William C. Velasquez Institute, titled *Color of Money: The 2004 Presidential Race*, found that 90% of those contributing more than $200 to federal political campaigns lived in predominantly white zip codes, more than half in well-off areas. Political investors representing just *one third of one percent* of the population contributed two thirds of all money from individuals. Manhattan's wealthy white Upper East Side led in what some called the "wealth election," one in which presidential and other political candidates must aggressively compete in our undemocratic system. It was more true than ever for the 2012 election.

When it comes to a cohesive, white male elite and its most sought-after political and economic goals (think of the federal bailout of Wall Street, even with its documented corruption and incompetence), President Obama has had to conform, no matter his personal desires. All presidents do that. Even in this new millennium, the predominantly white and male elite wins, fully controlling our still quite undemocratic, systemically racist, and oligarchical political and economic systems.

RECOMMENDED READING

Ronald Brownstein. 2007. *The Second Civil War: How Extreme Partisanship Has Paralyzed Washington and Polarized America*, New York: Penguin Group. A leading journalist assesses the increasing polarization of political parties and congressional caucuses in the United States.

Joe R. Feagin. 2012. *White Party, White Government: Race, Class, and U.S. Politics*, London: Routledge. Details the long history of systemic racism as it has shaped the evolution of U.S. politics and parties.

Adia Harvey-Wingfield and Joe R. Feagin. 2009. *Yes We Can: White Racial Framing and the 2008 Presidential Campaign*, London: Routledge. With a new edition on the way, this text examines the 2008 presidential campaigns and primaries with regard to the systemic racism that riddles recent campaign strategies and events.

Public Campaign, Fannie Lou Hamer Project, and William C. Velasquez Institute. October 2004. *Color of Money: The 2004 Presidential Race* (online resource). An excellent analysis of the role of money and wealth in U.S. presidential campaigns.

TSP tie-in

W hy do we listen to people with power? For many, this answer is one word: *authority*. What makes the right to wield power "justifiable," according to Max Weber, is the type of authority in question: charismatic, traditional, or legal-rational. Charismatic authority depends on the personal appeal of the leader. Think Barack Obama or, as one Sociological Images post suggests, Apple's Steve Jobs. Traditional authority rests on the appeal of the status quo—say, the authority of a long-standing monarchy or a well-established boarding school. Finally, Weber identified legal-rational authority, rooted in rules and the law. Legal-rational authority is highly routinized, rational, and often based on procedure. It is also thought to be particularly relevant in modern society.

Psychologist Stanley Milgram completed one of the most interesting and famous legal-rational authority experiments. Disturbed by the events of the Holocaust and curious about the extent to which people would follow orders—even ones that went against their usual moral inclinations—Milgram designed an experiment in which volunteers at his university would administer electric shocks to other volunteers. A scientist in the room would instruct the volunteers to shock the "subjects" up to lethal levels. As seen in the articles included at thesocietypages.org/politics, Milgram varied different aspects of the situation. In the end, he was surprised by the extent to which authority and situational context mattered in whether the volunteers balked at giving someone a deadly shock. With an authority figure—the scientist—on hand and in an "official" setting, more than 60% of the participants were willing to deliver the killer shock.

Similarly, Philip Zimbardo's Stanford Prison Experiment was designed to study the power of situations and the psychological effects of roles. Zimbardo chose twenty-four males who were deemed to be "psychologically average" and brought them to a mock prison. Half of the men were assigned to be "prisoners," and half were named "guards." Zimbardo hoped to learn how the men's assigned roles influenced their behavior, but he also studied the effects of authority—both his, as he took a role as the "superintendent" of the prison, and that of the guards. Soon after the experiment began, the guards started to abuse and dehumanize the prisoners. Many of the prisoners responded passively; the "guards" had, they believed, the authority to treat them this way. The experiment was scheduled to last two weeks, but Zimbardo called it off after just six days—another testament to the strength of authority and the situational context.

Browse thesocietypages.org/politics to read more about Weber's classifications of authority, the Milgram experiments, and Zimbardo's prison study.

HOLLIE NYSETH BREHM

cultural contexts

cultural contexts

the social functions of religion in american political culture

JOSEPH GERTEIS

Wrangling over the proper nature of the connection between politics and religion has been persistent and passionate since the Puritans first arrived in the new world. On the surface, today's division seems to be between a religious right and a secular left. It can also seem, especially from the point of view of the hyperpartisan political junkies of either side, that this division marks the difference between the sincere politicians who "get it" and those cynical ones who don't.

Early in the 2012 election cycle, religion really took center stage in political rhetoric and political news. Following the collapse of Rick Perry's and Michele Bachmann's Republican bids, those left in the running for their party's presidential nomination were jockeying to become the voice of religious conservatives. As I write, Rick Santorum has largely locked down that position and has been testing how his message might play out in the general election. For instance, in an apparent reference to environmental issues, Santorum said that President Obama adheres to "some phony theology. Not a theology based on the Bible. A different theology." On MSNBC, Santorum's press secretary referred to Obama's "radical Islamist policies" (she later said that she misspoke, while Santorum has added that if the president "says he's a Christian, he's a Christian").

It's tempting to chalk some of that rhetorical climate up to the depth of religious conviction among the crop of candidates, at least on the Republican side. Some of the credit (or blame) must also go to the larger political forces that select those candidates, especially the convergence of highly motivated religious and political actors among the self-styled religious right. But while religious beliefs and convictions are certainly real and candidates and their supporters may well mean everything they say about religion's role in political life, it turns out they couldn't get away from the topic even if they wanted to.

A great deal of work in recent years examines the institutional and organizational dimensions of religion in public life. I want to focus on the cultural role of religion. Specifically, I want to point out three social functions that have kept religion relevant in all eras of American politics (even as we espouse the separation of church and state), and how understanding these functions helps contextualize our political climate. In a nutshell, religion acts as a marker of trust, as a source of national solidarity, and a symbolic boundary of inclusion and exclusion. All three help reinforce political legitimacy.

religion as symbolic sincerity

In 1904, the well-known German social scientist Max Weber traveled to the United States, where he became particularly fascinated with the role of religion in American life. Weber later went on to write the most famous book in all of sociology, *The Protestant Ethic and the Spirit of Capitalism*. But during his visit, Weber also wrote a profound (but lesser known) essay called "The Protestant Sects and the Spirit of Capitalism" in which he attended to the symbolic and instrumental dimensions of religion.

He noticed that Americans always wanted, for instance, to proclaim their religious belonging in public settings. Why? Weber was no stranger to either public life or religion—his father was a German politician, his mother a devoutly religious woman, and Weber wrote a great deal about both politics and religion—but the public, political expression of religion in America baffled him.

"For some time in the United States a principled 'separation of state and church' has existed," he wrote. Yet, while Americans didn't care much about denomination (at least compared with the more doctrinaire Germans), church membership functioned as a marker of respectability and trust in business and political affairs. Weber came to the conclusion that American congregations—especially Methodists and Baptists—were essentially sects. Admission criteria for full membership in the congregation were high and served "as an absolute guarantee of the moral qualities of the gentleman." In this way, "sect membership meant a certificate of moral qualification and especially of business morals for the individual."

"Look at him . . . I told you so!" remarked a relative of Weber's living in North Carolina, upon witnessing the baptism of a man one cold morning. The relative explained that the man wanted to open a bank in the nearby county seat and would likely outcompete his rivals on the basis of his acceptance into the Baptist church. Weber was equally impressed on his journeys further West, when a businessman on a train explained that "for my part everybody may believe or not just as he pleases; but if I saw a farmer or businessman not belonging to any church at all, I wouldn't trust him with fifty cents. Why pay me, if he doesn't believe in anything?"

Above all, nineteenth-century American democracy was marked by a universalization of previously middle-class notions of respectability and belonging—the notion of community. And like the many community-based civic organizations of the time, religious organizations had a role to play in political life. "In the past and up to the present, it has been characteristic precisely of the specifically American democracy that it did *not* constitute a formless sand heap of individuals, but rather a buzzing complex of strictly exclusive, yet voluntary associations."

Exclusive, yet voluntary—no such community comes without exclusions. Weber thought Americans, to an almost comic extent, were far more likely to deny distinctions of social standing and status than Germans. Even still, an insistence on equality of status and equal belonging required conformity of views and conformity of norms, and it required markers of belonging. Religion, as Weber and everyday people observed, served as an American shorthand for trustworthiness.

religion as symbolic community

Weber's point was that part of the American tendency to proclaim religious affiliation in public is instrumental. We can understand why politicians might talk about religion in the same way we can understand why plumbers might put a Christian fish symbol on their work vans—it says, "I belong to this community. They trust me, and you can trust me too."

But that can't be the whole story. For a start, religious language and expression pervades all levels of civic and political life, going far beyond local communities of belonging. Even when these "communities" are really rather large categories—Republicans or the middle class—most political candidates have to try to connect with an even broader public in order to be successful.

More importantly, religion is not just a one-way cultural transmission from the candidates to the rest of us. Part of why religious language is so entrenched in American politics is that Americans demand it; the political expression of religious belief (or expressions of political belief couched in religious language) is an American norm. So, because religion provides a common tradition and frame of reference, it can also provide a common language for belonging. It is a basis for solidarity in our otherwise divided society.

The sociologist Robert Bellah popularized the term *civil religion* in the 1960s to capture this idea (it initially came from philosopher Jean-Jacques Rousseau). In an ostensibly secular society, religion nevertheless plays an important role in political life: it works both on a literal religious level and as a kind of public ritual. We *expect* presidents to invoke God in the State of the Union and inaugural addresses, not only as an expression of personal piety but also as an invocation of a higher power behind public life. Further, we expect it as an invocation of a common cultural background against which our differences can be, at least theoretically, harmonized. From this perspective, political religion is the public version of church rituals; it is the way we call our national community into being.

But this only works if we are more than just a "sand pile" of individuals, as Weber put it. In some of Bellah's later writing and in some recent work on the topic, the notion of civil religion has been called upon as a prescription as much as an explanation. What can bring us together in our increasingly polarized political climate and in our increasingly individualized civic life? If anything, perhaps civil religion, with its rhetoric of common belonging and its notion of American society as built on a covenant, can serve as a link between individual will and national destiny.

Of course, it is not just any kind of religious belief that signals belonging in this national "we." It has been, and remains, specifically Christian belonging that "counts." This itself is not eternal and unchanging: John Kennedy's Catholicism put him somewhat outside the mainstream in the early 1960s, and as I write this, two of the top Republican candidates for president have proudly proclaimed their Catholic faith. In the same way, we have seen the increasing, if still partial, embrace of the wider "Judeo-Christian" tradition in public rhetoric.

But Christianity, in its broadest form, is expected and indeed enforced. In a national survey, Doug Hartmann, Penny

Edgell, and I found that nearly 59% of Americans said that the United States was a "Christian country," and in a follow-up question they said that this was a positive thing. Another 17% said that it was not a Christian country, but it *should* be. Taken together, a majority of Americans held to this position across otherwise deep divides—rich and poor, black and white, Republican and Democrat. In the eyes of most Americans, being an American means being a Christian.

religion as symbolic boundary

Religion, then, can operate as a marker of belonging in specific communities and it can function as a platform for American belonging more generally. At one level, these are inclusive functions. But if Christianity plays such a central role in Americans' personal identities and in their understandings of the nation, why does religion seem to function in politics as a weapon as much as a common bond? The answer is that religion is a symbolic boundary, and like all boundaries, it both includes some and excludes others.

Some of this inclusion and exclusion works at a deep cultural level. It is often said that one can be almost anything, except an atheist, and still be president. While that may be an exaggeration, it is clear that belief is an expected part of American belonging (and, conversely, that nonbelievers do not belong). Opinion polls have long shown that atheists are at or near the bottom of the list of categories of people for whom Americans would be willing to choose as president. Similarly, nearly 40% of Americans told our research team that the degree to which atheists agree with "my view of American society" was "not at all." Most surprising was the fact that nearly 20% of people who reported themselves as completely nonreligious answered this way as well.

As it turns out, exclusion is related to the symbolic sincerity explored earlier. "How can I trust someone who doesn't believe in anything?" seems to be the way many people think about this. (And while atheists themselves presumably wouldn't think that way, look again at the ironic response of the "nonreligious" toward atheists.)

Going further, the specifically Christian nature of national political life leads to other kinds of exclusion from the American "we," despite the slowly expanding nature of that belonging. Next to atheists, Muslims are clearly the group most Americans think don't really belong. Representative Keith Ellison of Minnesota became the first Muslim member of the U.S. Congress, causing not just discomfort but outright hostility from some parts of the polity.

Finer distinctions also become apparent. Catholics have clearly broken through the kind of exclusion they faced in prior decades; Rick Santorum and Newt Gingrich, both

Catholics, were seen as acceptable candidates for most religious Republicans during the 2012 election. But what about Mitt Romney? His Mormon faith was not an overt issue in the campaign. However, it is not clear how much his relatively soft support was due to his personality, how much was due to his political positions, and how much was due to the fact that many were not sure about which side of the boundary Mormonism falls on.

what now for the culture war?

If we seem to be entering a particularly bloody religious skirmish in the American political culture war, there are also some reasons this war may be self-limiting. For one thing, recent decades of American history indicate a gradual but important expansion of the religious basis of the American "we"—from a narrowly Protestant understanding to one that includes Catholics and Jews, even if it still excludes Muslims and others. If we are not yet at a place where religious faith of any stripe is a marker of belonging, it seems that we are trending that way. The simple fact that the Judeo-Christian tradition has come to replace the Christian-only tradition so widely may mean that Americans will be unwilling to draw boundaries too strongly among believers for much longer.

This is not the first time in American history that populist politics (especially now in the Tea Party) have tracked the rise of religious distinctions in politics. At the turn of the twentieth century, populism involved significant anti-Catholic and anti-Semitic views. The oddity of the 2012 election was that those on the Republican side who were most willing to push religion as a political issue and castigate Democrats as "secularists" were two Catholics and a Mormon, while the sitting Democratic president had long since been involved with a historically black Protestant church (one that was somewhat out of step with the mainstream in its own attention to worldly issues of race), but is frequently accused of being a secret Muslim. Even when formally separate, religion and politics have a way of overlapping in the American imagination.

————

As a broad generalization, Democratic and Republican politicians do tend to draw on religion in different ways: Democrats tend to see religion an important but essentially private matter, whereas Republicans tend to see it as public. But this is not exactly right, and certainly not when we are talking about the public at large. As the sociologist Christian Smith has pointed out, evangelical Christians are not a monolithic group. The high level of religious commitment of both Democrats and Republicans means effectively that religion is not likely to leave the public sphere. It also means that Americans may be wary any time it becomes too tightly connected to the profane world of partisan battles. As de Tocqueville observed long ago, the formal separation of church and state has served the interests of both religious and political institutions.

RECOMMENDED READINGS

Will M. Gervais, Azim F. Shariff, and Ara Norenzayan. 2011. "Do You Believe in Atheists? Distrust Is Central to Anti-atheist Prejudice," *Journal of Personality and Social Psychology* 101(6):1189–1206. One of the most recent examples of a wave of new social psychology on the social sources of anti-atheist sentiment in North American life.

James Guth, John Green, Corwin Smith, and Lyman Kellstedt. 1994. "It's the Culture, Stupid!" *First Things* 42(1):28–33. A now-classic piece about cultural coalitions in American electoral politics focusing on the 1992 presidential election.

Darren Sherkat. 2005. "Politics and Social Movements," in *Handbook of Religion and Social Institutions* (pp. 1–18), edited by Helen Rose Ebaugh. New York: Springer Science and Business Media, Inc. An expansive overview of social scientific research on religion and movements that emphasizes religion, including a section on religion and exclusion.

Christian Smith. 2000. *Christian America? What Evangelicals Really Want*, Berkeley: University of California Press. A well-known study of American Evangelicals that proposes a sub-cultural identity theory of religious persistence in the modern world that highlights the cultural paradoxes of conservative Protestantism.

Kenneth D. Wald and David C. Leege. 2010. "Mobilizing Religious Differences in American Politics," in *Religion and Democracy in the United States: Danger or Opportunity?* (pp. 355–381), edited by Alan Wolfe and Ira Katznelson. Princeton, NJ: American Political Science Association/Princeton University Press. A comprehensive and constructive synthesis of political science research in the area.

Max Weber. 1904. "The Protestant Sects and the Spirit of Capitalism." This classic essay focuses on the key symbolic and social functions of religious affiliations.

politics and sports: strange, secret bedfellows

KYLE GREEN AND DOUGLAS HARTMANN

So, are you more Super Bowl or Super Tuesday? No matter how you answer, if you are like most Americans, you probably think the two—sports and politics—are unrelated. You might even object to the suggestion of a tie on principle alone. We're not so bold as to suggest there aren't some good reasons for the separation of sport and politics, but this orientation is, in certain ways, unfortunate. It can blind us to the ways in which the two contested fields are intimately bound together in contemporary American culture. Sport scholars and cultural critics have actually spent a good deal of time thinking about and researching these relationships over the years. Academics like us have looked at politics in sports and sports in politics. In this piece, we take a look at the latter—that is, the ways in which sports are part of and implicated in the political process. It is an exploration that not only shows the power of sport in politics but also challenges and expands some of our basic conceptions of politics itself.

sports and political leadership

Barack Obama was proclaimed the "Sports President" even before he set foot in the White House. Sport pundits wrote glowingly of the potential for positive change that Obama's election would bring: the power of players' unions would be increased, Title IX would be enforced, the Olympics would come to Chicago and the World Cup to American soil, and the long-criticized college football bowl system would finally be repaired. While many of the loftier expectations have not been met, Obama *has* maintained the label by regularly attending sporting events of all types, inviting his favorite teams to the White House, showing off his jump shot during frequent games of pickup basketball, and sharing his annual video explanation of his March Madness picks (a video that occupies a prime spot on ESPN's home page every year).

As we write in mid-2012, the celebration of Obama seems to be a case of collective amnesia. Only a few years ago, George W. Bush was hailed as the "Sports President" due to his own sporting pedigree—the one-time owner of the Texas Rangers, he took outspoken pride in throwing out the first pitch at the World Series in post-9/11 New York and had a passion for running, biking, and working out. And before Bush, Bill Clinton was frequently spotted cheering on his Arkansas Razorbacks or out on the golf green, and he was lauded for his involvement in Major League baseball negotiations. And before Clinton, much was made of the first President Bush's baseball career at Yale. In fact, if we peruse the historical archives, it seems almost every president was hailed with the same title. Other "Sports Presidents" included Gerald Ford, the All-American center from Michigan; Richard Nixon, a former college football player who loved to spend time at the bowling alley and even drew up a play for the Washington Redskins; JFK, who was famous for his swimming ability and fitness; and Teddy Roosevelt, who, well known for his rugged lifestyle, boxed and wrestled in the White House and introduced rules to increase the safety of college football. Obama wasn't our first "Sports President," nor do we suspect he'll be the last.

Social scientists haven't spent as much time researching these connections as you might expect. Perhaps it is because the appearance of political leaders at local sporting events is so deeply normalized that we don't even notice it. However, as any good sociologist will tell you, sometimes that which seems the most ordinary is the most revealing. In this case, a critical examination reveals sport serving at least three key functions.

First, sport provides a stage for public visibility, attention, and awareness. For a politician, virtually all publicity is good. Appearing at an event, whether throwing out the first pitch of a big game or simply sitting in the stands, is bound to attract cameras and a mention in the local newspaper. At the very minimum, sport provides a safe stage for a politician to remind the public of her existence.

Second and more significantly, sport can help solidify a politician's reputation, identity, and social status. It can demonstrate that a politician is, at least on some level, just one of the guys (or gals)—or even better: a *certain* kind of guy (or gal). Sociologists, in particular French theorist Pierre Bourdieu, have argued that taste plays a key role in dividing social groups. When a politician appears at, say, a college basketball game, it shows they share a common passion with the wider public. In the same way a political candidate drinking a beer at the local watering hole has become an obligatory photo-op, appearing at a sporting event proves he or she isn't an elitist snob.

And much like it is important that the candidate knows *how* to hold the pint glass in the photo-op at the bar, it is important the politician act like an "ordinary sports fan" at the game. Both the politician's emotions and favorite team's colors should be worn for all to see. When Obama makes a joke at the expense of the Packers, the rival of his hometown Bears, it doesn't alienate Green Bay fans (in fact, it endears them) because he is acting in the appropriate manner—he's acting like a real sports fan. This creates the all-important space for an emotional connection to be made.

Of course, sport, like the bar, has a long tradition as masculine space; sometimes it's even characterized as a "refuge of masculinity." This provides yet another barrier to women seeking success in the political realm, another of the "last refuges."

In any case, the manner in which sport provides the chance to connect with communities that bridge political and ideological divides makes it particularly appealing to those seeking public approval. This speaks to the third way in which sport is crucial to political leadership. Whether it is sitting courtside or receiving athletic champions at the White House, politicians love to be associated with the fun, positive energy associated with modern sports, not to mention the aura of excellence, excitement, and success. These appearances work toward the creation of legitimacy, likeability, and credibility through the transference of the positive feelings associated with sports, especially those that are popular and successful.

There isn't much research on the mechanisms through which this transfer works, but there is little doubt that smart politicians and their advisors are constantly on the lookout for opportunities to create good feelings by associating their campaigns and agendas with athletes and athletic events (albeit cautiously—political types can never be too overt about any of this, lest they violate the ideals and values that both domains hold dear).

The same tactics are used by many: for years, researchers have documented the massive capital corporations have invested to build associations with popular teams or athletes. For example, sport researchers Stephen Jackson and Jay Scherer have written on the relationship between Adidas and New Zealand's dominant rugby squad, the All Blacks, and the scholar Walter LaFeber documented the global reach of the Nike-Michael Jordan alliance. Just as athletes and athletic associations sell products, politicians try to associate with sport to help sell themselves and their agendas to a sport-loving public.

the politics of sport and culture

Usually when Americans talk about politics they are referring to campaigns and elections, legislative debates, and the making of law and public policy. Surely the emphasis on electoral processes organizes how much of academic political science is oriented. But there is another, broader aspect of political life that is easy to overlook or leave out. This is what we might call cultural politics. The politics of culture involve how political communities and interests are created, consolidated, and maintained; it involves the construction of cultural frames and social problems—what are seen as problems in need of attention or correction, what is considered core to the public interest, and what's not even worthy of political consideration.

Some of the most famous scholars of sport have spent their time theorizing from this perspective, examining how sport is central to creating and reinforcing social solidarities and collective identities, what is seen as natural or acceptable (and thus not open to political action or contestation), and which social problems are most pressing.

The ever-elusive notion of "community" provides a prime illustration. In recent years, politicians and academics have bemoaned the decline in community pride and civic attachment. And perhaps it is true that more people are now bowling alone, as Robert Putnam's book claims; however, the number of people tailgating before the big game, united by their love of *their* team, has only grown. The founders of the sociological discipline were driven by the question of what would bring people together and serve as a unifying force in a society that was rapidly becoming more complicated, diverse, and fragmented. In many places, for better or worse, sport has been the answer. Sport provides a public activity that is often as much about the audience as the participants. In doing so, a basis for some sort of common, unified, and collective identity is provided.

The community fervor that can surround sport is well captured in H. G. Bissinger's popular book *Friday Night Lights* (on high school football in a small Texas town) and is the subject of insightful analysis in Richard Gruneau and David Whitson's *Hockey Night in Canada*. Arguments for the public funding of professional sport stadiums rely heavily on the belief that sport can forge community. Plus, building such monuments to sports is one of the few endeavors a local politician can undertake to define her agenda and leave her mark on a city.

Sport and culture studies of the cultural dimensions of the politics surrounding sport, though, have tended to focus on sport's conservative or reproductive social nature. From this perspective, sport is an institution that tends to reproduce the existing social status quo, and, in that way, it can work on behalf of those politicians or political parties currently in office. More than this, it reproduces current class divisions as well as understandings of race, gender, and sexuality by making current social standings seem both organic and set.

In the most extreme reading, sport serves as what a Marxist might call the "opiate of the masses"—something mindless to occupy the working class's time and energy, which might otherwise be invested in creating drastic political change. Studies in this tradition have become more nuanced through engagement with the work of classic social theorist Antonio Gramsci, a move that has led to sport being conceived of as a site of contestation and potential resistance. However, even with the added complexity, the political significance of sport remains rooted in its role in the reproduction of social class.

Race scholars have questioned the role sport plays in maintaining racial stereotypes, in particular the athletic prowess and intellectual deficiency of black men. Ben Carrington, in his recent book *Race, Sport, and Politics,* adds to this literature through a specific focus on how sport has been a central site for both establishing and resisting understandings of race and biological difference. In his work, Carrington illustrates that sport is able to play such a significant role in the construction of racial images and identities because of the common (but misplaced) perception that it is located in an apolitical realm.

Feminist theorists take much the same view, conceptualizing sport as a key site for the reproduction of understandings of gender. Drawing heavily on French cultural theorist Michel Foucault, gender scholars have examined how the body itself becomes a political site upon which power operates. Debates over the value of Title IX and the effectiveness of the sex testing performed by athletic commissions demonstrates how sporting institutions both rely on and help establish a binary understanding of gender. Similarly, many of the most important of the masculinity scholars, including Raewyn Connell, Michael Messner, and Michael Kimmel, have highlighted sport as a central site where boys learn how to perform a dominant, physical brand of manhood.

Because of its cultural prominence and the ways in which it is bound up with so many of the differences and inequalities of contemporary society, activists (both in and around sport) have often seen sport as a potential arena for contestation and change. Whether considering the 1968 African American Olympic protests or Title IX gender equity activism, sport scholars (including ourselves) have devoted a tremendous amount of energy and attention to these potentials and possibilities. This is, in fact, the single most familiar use and meaning of the terms *politics* and *sports* in the field: protests, activism, social movements using sport to call attention to existing inequalities, and working on behalf of broader social change.

But for all of this, the fact of the matter is that sport's political effects would seem to be far more powerful as a means of social reproduction, in maintaining the social order as it is. Sport tends to be associated with political antichange, the maintenance of the status quo. And perhaps the most obvious and yet least appreciated example of that involves the display of anthems, flags, and even military personnel (or fighter jets) at sporting events large and small, local and international.

Sport has long been a means of establishing national pride and a belief in a population's genetic or at least cultural superiority. When boxer Joe Louis avenged his earlier loss to Max Schmeling with a first-round knockout it was considered a victory for American democracy over a perverted German nationalism, not just one boxer over another. The importance placed on American Olympic athletes' success during the Cold War provides yet another example. Significantly, they were under pressure not only to win medals, but also to unite the population in celebration of both athletic and moral superiority.

spotting sport in political discourse

A third area in which sports and politics are deeply implicated, perhaps even inextricably woven together, is within political discourse, so much of which is informed by and expressed through sports metaphors and images.

Sport historians and theorists have debated which political regimes in the history of the modern world have been best positioned and able to make political use of sport. What stands out about sport in American politics (if not in other liberal democracies as well) is the way in which sport's idealized culture of competitive fair play mirrors, matches, and models American conceptions of justice, fairness, and the good society.

Unlike the ability to down a local brew, sport is also associated with *moral* worth. Within the popular media and the community of fans, the sporting world is cherished as meritocracy at its finest. The playing field is said to be even, and the players who reach the highest levels do so through talent, drive, and hard work. As a fan, it is nearly impossible to avoid subscribing to these omnipresent ideals. Tales of players "pulling themselves up by their bootstraps" and escaping abject poverty to achieve incredible wealth based on being the hardest worker on the team dominate ESPN's "color commentary" and the pages of *Sports Illustrated*. And on the field, cooperation, cohesion, reciprocity, and self-sacrifice are celebrated as essential to bringing team success. When it works, all of this individualism and hard work and team play fits together so seamlessly and smoothly that it seems like it couldn't be any other way—and that any failing is just one's own, personal shortcoming.

This can be positive and problematic. On the positive side, the idea that sport is somehow a model or metaphor for social life makes it a frequent reference point, either in terms of abstract ideas, ideals, and values or in terms of athletes, competitions, and events in the sporting world being believed to embody and used to express political and ideological views. To be seen as possessing those upstanding qualities through association can provide a powerful vehicle for sending those messages (not to mention an all-so-important boost in the public opinion polls). On the negative side, the infusion of sports language and metaphors in politics can be seen to undermine politics itself—making it less serious about real issues, more cutthroat and competitive, more about process than about outcomes and people.

In his book on sports, race, and the Olympics, Douglas Hartmann looked at how Ronald Reagan talked about the Olympic torch relay in the context of his reelection campaign of 1984. On the one hand, Reagan waxed poetic about the torch relay in an attempt to capitalize on the patriotic enthusiasm and exuberance that surrounded the spectacular American performance in the 1984 Los Angeles Olympics (boycotted by the USSR and its Eastern Bloc allies).

But a closer read of the speech reveals that Reagan's emphasis on the Olympic torch relay was about much more than building public support for his presidency and his reelection campaign. The President also used the event to craft and convey his unique, post-1960s vision of social justice and racial harmony. It was a vision that was based on individual opportunity and a community in which individuals (not groups) were united around a common cause, had equal access to opportunity, and drew heavily if implicitly on the ideals about fair play, competition, hard work, and individual effort that circulate widely within the world of sport itself. It was a moving portrait, a stirring vision made all the more powerful by the fact that many who heard it thought of it as nothing more than a story about an all-American event, a set of ideals that any and every American could agree upon.

seeing through a sacred divide

It does not take a great imagination, only a sociological one, to see that sport is a powerful political platform. Sport is actively sought as a stage on which to be seen and solidify one's public identity, political legitimacy, and leadership qualities. It is important in reproduction of social categories. Sports language and imagery is pervasive in our political rhetoric. There is no denying it, from paying for new stadiums through public tax dollars to standing for the national anthem to considering a mandate that women boxers must wear skirts, politics and sport are tightly intertwined.

Some might take these observations as the impetus to, once and for all, get sport out of politics (and politics out of sports)—either because sport is believed to be above all the political scrum (a sacred realm of sorts) or simply better understood as a realm of fun and entertainment that is only compromised by the complexity and conflict of real-world politics. This isn't necessarily our goal. Instead, we simply seek to call attention to the fact that in the real world sport and politics are not nearly as separate as we might think or would like to believe.

That said, we also realize our modest goal has some potentially far-reaching implications that might first be understood and imagined. We don't want to sell it short.

Sport is a powerful and important political force. But it is most powerful when people are least aware of it—when people believe that nothing important or unusual is going on; in other words, when the politics are hidden or masked, seen as natural or organic. For politicians, this means that they must engage in a delicate dance. Even as they use sport for a political purpose, it is essential that sport retain its status as a somehow sacred or at least special space. For the rest of us, this means trying to be aware of what is going on in order that we might participate in both politics and sports with our eyes open, as equals rather than as dupes subject to the manipulation and exploitation of others.

The point, in short, is that it's not necessary to take sport out of politics, but simply to realize that it is there and to engage it appropriately. Perhaps this realization is the first and most basic "political" act of all.

RECOMMENDED READING

Richard Gruneau and David Whitson. 1994. *Hockey Night in Canada: Sport, Identities, and Cultural Politics*, Toronto, ON, Canada: University of Toronto Press, Garamond. An exemplary, multifaceted study of the cultural politics of sport in Canada.

Jennifer Hargreaves. 2000. *Heroines of Sport: The Politics of Difference and Identity*, New York: Taylor & Francis. The cultural politics of sport and gender, from a leading feminist in the field.

John Hoberman. 1984. *Sport and Political Ideology*, Austin: University of Texas Press. A classic exploration of the affinities between sports and political orientations and regimes ranging from communism and socialism to fascism, authoritarianism, and liberal democracy.

John J. MacAloon. 1987. "Missing Stories: American Politics and Olympic Discourse." *Gannett Center Journal* (Columbia University) Fall 1(2):111–142. A provocative commentary on the peculiar structure and function of the Olympics in American political discourse.

John Sayle Watterson. 2006. *The Games Presidents Play: Sports and the Presidency*, Baltimore, MD: The Johns Hopkins University Press. The most useful historical overview of the subject available.

facebook's impact on american politics

JOSE MARICHAL

To the extent that political scientists evaluate Facebook's impact on the American political system, the verdict is that it doesn't matter much, particularly when compared with other factors like the condition of the economy or number of combat casualties (see Chapter 13). And this assessment might be true if we gauge impact via a direct, measurable effect on electoral outcomes. But what if Facebook impacts politics in a much broader way? Here, I look at how the site's nearly ubiquitous use might change not just the outcome of the political game, but the playing field itself.

In October 2012, Facebook surpassed one billion accounts. In a 2010 blog post, its researchers reported they could predict the winning House candidate over 70% of the time, just by looking at the candidates' "likes." While Facebook has a vested interest in convincing the mass public that it has its "finger on the pulse" of mass culture, social scientists have a great deal of skepticism regarding its impact on the political process. As Gregory Ferenstein recently posted on Tech-Crunch, "if social media mattered in elections, Ron Paul would have a realistic shot at being the Republican nominee." Indeed, one only has to compare the significant gap in Facebook page "likes" between President Obama (31,129,331 on October 22, 2012) and Republican candidate Mitt Romney (10,330,215 on the same day) to their much closer positions in the polls to recognize that Facebook popularity contests aren't directly translatable to electoral outcomes.

Another key argument against Facebook's impact on American politics is that those most likely to use Facebook are also least likely to be engaged with politics. A May 2012 Pew survey found that close to two thirds of people in the United States reported using some form of social media and almost all of those used Facebook. When broken down by age, 86% of 18- to 29-year-olds used social networking sites. By comparison, only 34% of those 65 and older were social networking site users. Since 18- to 29-year-olds are histori-cally less likely to vote than other groups, Facebook would not appear to be very fertile soil from which to extract votes. Shoring up this idea, a recent Gallup survey affirmed that 18- to 30-year-olds were significantly less engaged in the 2012 presidential election than they had been in 2008.

But Facebook can't be blamed for the public cynicism that stems from partisan gridlock in Washington. Some argue that Facebook might be affecting politics by ushering in a new, different era of youth participation. So, though young voters might be less likely to vote in elections, Facebook users are "civically engaged" in other ways. A 2011 Pew Internet and American Life survey found that frequent Facebook users (that is, those who visited the site at least once a day) were more likely to exhibit a number of procivic attitudes. They were three times as likely as nonusers to believe that people could be trusted, had closer personal ties, and were more likely to receive social, emotional, and tangible support from friends. These "connected" Facebook citizens exhibited greater levels of the social capital that sociologist Robert Putnam and others see as vital to civic life, which generally means they are more likely to engage in public life than be disconnected from it.

Furthermore, the same 2011 Pew survey found that frequent Facebook users were much more politically active than nonusers. These frequent users were 53% more likely to vote than nonmembers or infrequent users, 78% more likely to try to influence someone to vote, and over two and a half times more likely to attend a political meeting or rally.

So, is Facebook a vital engine for promoting civic engagement? Perhaps, but major questions of cause and correlation remain. Do civically and politically engaged people become heavy Facebook users, or does heavy Facebook use make users more politically engaged? Maybe what matters is not how often people use Facebook, but the ways in which they engage.

Scholars Moira Burke and Robert Kraut, along with Facebook researcher Cameron Marlow, have found that Facebook users increase their level of social capital when they engage in direct, person-to-person communication with Facebook friends. Similarly, social scientists Namsu Park, Kerk F. Kee, and Sebastian Valenzuela have shown that students who use Facebook to socialize with friends or seek information are more likely to become engaged in politics than those who just use it for entertainment. And, in a 2009 talk, Jessica T. Feezell, Meredith Conroy, and Mario Guerrero reported that college students who belonged to a Facebook group were more engaged with politics and more likely to vote than those who were not. It appears that those who seek out political information on Facebook find it and are more likely to engage in politics that those Facebook users who don't, but whether Facebook creates politically engaged citizens is very different matter.

Evgeny Morozov's 2011 book *The Net Delusion* provides a withering critique of the transformational possibilities of the Internet in general, but Facebook in particular. He suggests that the ease with which users can express sympathy with social causes through "like" and "share" buttons leads to what he calls "slacktivism." Once one can identify with a social cause at a distance, there is little incentive to get directly involved in the serious and coordinated work of social change. Malcolm Gladwell made a similar argument in an October 2010 *New Yorker* article, claiming that Facebook connections were based on "weak" ties rather than the "strong" social connections needed to sustain social change. Gladwell cited sociologist Doug McAdam's 1986 finding that activists in the civil rights movement were personally affected by racism and discrimination and that this personal attachment sustained the movement's intensity. Since Facebook is based on a network model, whereas sustained social movements require some level of hierarchical organization, movements formed on Facebook will be too diffuse to produce lasting change.

In my own research, I come to a similar conclusion, but for different reasons. In my book, *Facebook Democracy*, I examined 250 political Facebook groups. Few had been created for the purpose of mobilization, but this was not because of weak ties—in fact, rather than simply promote weak ties, Facebook seemed to amplify or dampen both the weak *and* strong tie bonds we form offline. Facebook can accommodate a whole range of different types of network formations. As James Fowler and Nickolas Christakis noted in their popular 2010 book *Connected*, individual networks can be small, long lasting, populated by like-minded people, and dense, or they can be large, diffuse, and highly diverse. So it is that Facebook networks range from the college student who "friends" a stranger from halfway around the world to the husband who "updates" his wife to pick up a carton of milk from the supermarket. There is no one type of network formation that predominates on Facebook (and it is this diversity of network formations that makes Facebook so appealing for so many).

Why so little emphasis on mobilizing? Because Facebook emphasizes connection and disclosure over other forms of political discourse. And what happens when political discourse is about connection and disclosure? It effectively privatizes the public sphere. By taking the inherently intimate and personal act of disclosing to and connecting with others and putting it in what looks to Facebook users like a public forum, all sorts of conversations become personal, whether they should be or not. If the public sphere is about the objective social, economic, and political world we all share, what philosopher Hannah Arendt (1958) calls the "world of things," the private/market sphere (like the one Facebook creates) is about the personal pursuit of self-interest.

I find that the majority of political groups on Facebook are "informational," intended to exercise political voice. For example, a page called "Ronald Reagan" was created specifically to show admiration for the former U.S. president. The creation of such a Facebook page is not intended to help users engage in a collective search for "the truth," it's an exercise in disclosing affinity and connecting with similar others. In effect, it is about "performing political identity." This type of discourse is particularly prevalent on Facebook. One can hardly imagine someone bothering to stand on a street corner holding a sign stating that they support a president who hasn't held office for over twenty years.

Media critic Lincoln Dahlberg noted that the great promise of the Internet was creating online rhetorical spaces that were free of elite control. This personalization of political discourse also necessarily focuses on those policy issues that are easy to translate into the personal language of feelings. It is much easier to process how one feels about Missouri Senate candidate Todd Akin's "legitimate rape" assertions than it is to personalize the Greek debt crisis.

Personalization is not unique to Facebook: it exacerbates a long-term trend in Western democracies toward making the political world more intimate. Television has played a significant role in making candidate appearance and presentation of self matter as much as rhetorical content for candidate evaluations. But by personalizing and privatizing the public sphere, Facebook makes it harder to create "free" spaces, not because it is formally controlling discourse, but because discourse is driven toward subjects that are easily translatable into "feelings" that can be "performed" on Facebook.

This emphasis on disclosure is not restricted to homogeneous networks. Facebook is not, as Eli Pariser suggests, a "filter bubble" in which we can tune out dissonant voices. In Pariser's book, the current board president of activist group MoveOn.org argues Facebook is one of a number of social applications that encourage users to live in a content bubble, where they are easily able to filter out information that doesn't reinforce their preexisting beliefs. If that's true, Facebook would exacerbate our already built-in tendency to group around ideological "tribes." In reality, Facebook users have more diverse networks that we might presume: Facebook isn't a political blog like Daily Kos or Red State. Facebook connections are primarily formed around social/geographic proximity, not shared interests like on other parts of the Web. As such, Facebook is less likely to promote individual filter bubbles than other sites.

Granted, social proximity and shared interest overlap to some degree: people in the same upper-income neighborhood are likely to share similar interests. However, this overlap is less pronounced when it comes to political attitudes. Sharad Goel and his colleagues at Yahoo! found that Facebook friends were more homophilous in their political views than random groups, but the difference (75% agreement for Facebook friends vs. 63% for randomly assigned groups) was marginal, albeit statistically significant. Perhaps more curious than whether individuals are exposed to diverse views on Facebook is the fact that Facebook appears to be a generally apolitical forum. As Goel and his colleagues noted, Facebook users

> are probably surrounded by a greater diversity of opinions than is sometimes claimed, [but they] generally fail to talk about politics, and that when they do, they simply do not learn much from their conversations about each other's views ... the extent to which peers influence each other's political attitudes may be less than is sometimes claimed.

This is the main problem with "talk" on Facebook. Because of its structure, the social networking site encourages the performance of political identity over deliberation. But discourse like this doesn't reflect or encourage a collective search for the truth or a particularly effective preparation for democratic citizenship. Identity formation is only a stage in the political process, so Facebook, as a business, has no interest in the transition of a public political identity into a public citizen engaged in political life. In fact, having a political identity or a political opinion is not politics. Politics is about engaging in a collective conversation about how we should pursue the good life. That collective conversation does not mean some fantasy town hall where every citizen is completely open-minded and engaged with the issues. But it does mean actively engaging in the political arena and recognizing that public life in a democratic society is about accepting a set of ground rules for the greater public good.

In another argument for Facebook as the great democratizer, Facebook makes your representative more available to you. At first blush, it seems to present constituents with unprecedented opportunities to access political information and to do constituency service. Facebook as a medium, though, demands that politicians seem "authentic" and compels them to "disclose" and "connect." The very notion of "following" or "liking" one's senator connotes a personalization of the constituent/representative relationship, though, so this personalization of politics, this demand for authenticity, means politicians need to appeal to emotion, not policy. Politicians move away from a collective search for the truth (or, at least, a productive political conversation) and toward easy appeals and emotional responses to policy issues.

Sometimes such personalization is essential. Facebook's effect in galvanizing the 2011 Egyptian revolution, for example, is undeniable. A Facebook page called We Are All Khalid Said, created to memorialize an Egyptian citizen killed by police, served as a site for everyday Egyptians to express collective dissent. Here, and in other places, Facebook can provide a vehicle for the personal expression of political views, especially where individuals' rights are constrained. It is particularly in places that don't have respect for the individual that individual "voice" matters. However, an overemphasis on the personal in rights-based societies filters politics through feelings rather than emphasizing politics through the lens of a collective search for pragmatic truth.

In democratic states in which voice is guaranteed by law, listening, rather than expressing, becomes an equally important quality. Early utopian thinking about the Web posited it as a radical public sphere (Salter, 2005) where alternative voices could be heard. But unlike blogs with discrete URLs, Facebook does not provide independent pieces of Internet real estate. Instead, Facebook corrals all these voices in one place. Even in Egypt, listening was necessary to foment revolution. Social scientist Barry Wellman and his colleagues highlight how the seeds of the revolution were sown by Egyptian bloggers who fostered a "networked public sphere" of social critics. Without this community of voices providing spaces for political deliberation, the Khalid Said Facebook page would have had little effect.

In the U.S., balancing more voices with more listening remains crucial for democracy to flourish. If Facebook's main purpose is to enhance social connection, then controversial (e.g., political) subjects run the risk of inhibiting the formation of these bonds. This is where I think Facebook has the largest impact upon politics. Facebook encourages a further privatization and personalization of the civic sphere—a place that is inherently public, and in which everyone should both express personal identity and come together to deliberate over the good life.

What does all this mean for elections? It means that, on Facebook at least, we are likely to talk about how we "feel" about pressing political issues and politicians, rather than the issues themselves. Political figures exacerbate this trend by personalizing themselves. Knowing whether President Obama likes Stevie Wonder *should* be less relevant than whether his proposal for remedying income inequality is likely to be effective, but Facebook exacerbates a trend toward political personalization of politics. Still, it offers a great many elements that make it advantageous for politics. In the 2010 book *Digital Activism Decoded*, Mary Joyce and her contributors found that many grassroots organizations rely on Facebook to promote their cause and coordinate activities. While Facebook's disappointing initial public offering may have dampened some of the enthusiasm over its transformative possibilities, this one giant site is not the end of the social media story. New social media tools like Twitter, Pinterest, and Google+ are on the rise. These might provide alternative models of communication that enhance public discourse in ways that Facebook cannot.

RECOMMENDED READING

Matthew Hindman. 2007. *The Myth of Digital Democracy*, Princeton, NJ: Princeton University Press. An empirical analysis that challenges the notion that the Internet enhances the diversity of political discourse.

Rebecca MacKinnon. 2012. *Consent of the Networked: The Worldwide Struggle for Internet Freedom*, New York: Basic Books. Clearly highlights the subtle way authoritarian systems use the Internet to maintain power.

Evgeny Morozov. 2011. *The Net Delusion: The Dark Side of Internet Freedom*, New York: Public Affairs. An important critique of the impact of Facebook and the Internet on promoting liberty and fostering social movement mobilization.

Zizi Paparachizzi. 2010. *A Networked Self: Identity, Community, and Culture on Social Network Sites*, London: Routledge. An excellent analysis of how the Internet changes the nature of social relations and our individual self-presentations.

Eli Pariser. 2011. *The Filter Bubble: What the Internet Is Hiding from You*, New York: Penguin. A useful practitioner analysis of how Facebook and the Internet personalize everyday life for users.

9

laughter and the political landscape

SARAH LAGESON, SINAN ERENSU, AND KYLE GREEN

Making fun of politicians is a fundamental part of American culture—particularly as we race toward each major election. As this group of scholars points out, political humor is unique in its ability to humanize and criticize, while also creating serious political and social commentary through satire, stand-up, and other comedic forms. Social science helps untangle the meanings and effects of American political humor.

What are the dominant forms and persistent themes of political humor?

Kristen Landreville: Popular venues for political humor today include late-night comedy shows and satirical websites. While oftentimes the humor focuses on more trivial matters, such as a politician's appearance or personality, political humor also has a serious side that sometimes provides serious political, social, or economic commentary. It is this type of political humor that politicians, institutions, and authority figures over the centuries have feared the most. For example, satire . . . can make politicians nervous because of [its] attacks on their character, policy, or even larger issues like the electoral system. . . . The cogs start spinning in people's minds, and, soon enough, people begin to deeply question a particular politician, authority figure, or group.

History shows us that politicians have been persistently cautious, and sometimes hostile, to political humor and satire. Plato saw satire as a type of magic that needed legal penalties. In early Rome, emperors banned satire and employed a punishment of death to satirists. British authority also banned it during the Middle Ages. You get the point: It's tough to be an authority figure and love political satire.

Don Waisanen: I think the label "humor" can often gloss over an incredibly rich diversity of comedic forms. For instance, some political humor is based upon exaggerating characters, imitating an individual's physical tics, quirky mannerisms, or unreflective slogans—such as Stephen Colbert's parody of combative media figures.

On the other hand, comedians like Jon Stewart are more satirical . . . primarily attacking substance rather than style. . . . [A] as soon as a statement might be made about dominant types of humor, we find examples of evasive and evolving comedy that defy traditional categories. Some comics now even create humor through a type of paradoxical "anticomedy." Fred Armisen's bad political comedian character on *Saturday Night Live* is one such example.

Bruce Williams: [W]e live in a world now where professional journalists speaking through newspapers and network news broadcasts have lost a lot of their authority to shape the kind of language and narrative of politics in the United States. Now . . . political information is coming at us through a bewildering number of conduits [and] individuals are much more able to shape the kind of media diet they consume. . . . That's a very different situation than by the end of the 1980s, when eight out of every ten television sets that were turned on were watching one of the three nightly news broadcasts, not because people were more committed or were better citizens then, but because it was the only thing on!

Jon Stewart has to attract and keep his audience every single night. . . . [O]ne of the concepts that I am most skeptical about is the idea that there somehow is a sharp distinction between news and entertainment or between serious stuff and stuff that's less serious or fluffy.... [H]umor ... is just one of the ways in which, in a fragmented market, providers of information or people who want to comment on the political world can attract and maintain an audience.... [T]he context is different even if the kinds of humor that get deployed are not that different.

What are the limits to what's "appropriate" to joke about in politics?

Robert (Lance) Holbert: There are some classic rules that apply to joke telling in general that are also applicable to politics. For example, there are certain political events that require some time or emotional distance before humorous perspectives can be offered about them. This issue was made salient after the 9/11 tragedies. This issue is a classic one concerning the tragedy-comedy dichotomy—when can we make the switch from tragedy to comedy?

As for satire, this question speaks to the issue of effectiveness. When will a piece of satire be well received and deemed to have possible influence on a public? One perspective offered on this matter argues that there needs to be an implicit agreement between the satirist and the satiree (i.e., the audience member consuming the satire) that the subject of the satirical material (i.e., the satirized) is worthy of satirization. Two questions are usually raised when judging worthiness: (1) Has the person being satirized made choices that have led them to being a public figure? and (2) Is the characteristic of the person being satirized a genuine example of human folly/weakness? If you can answer in the affirmative on both counts, then the object is worthy of possible satirization. So, there can be a satirical piece about President Obama and how he often thinks very highly of his intellectual abilities (i.e., hubris as human weakness). However, a piece of satire about the President's daughters, who have not chosen to be public figures, and their academic performance would be deemed off limits for a majority of the American public.

Landreville: The limits are perpetually being tested and redrawn. Comedians and satirists push the limits of commentary on religion, race, capitalism, gender identity, sexual affiliation, the political system, stereotypes, and a myriad of other topics that parents typically teach their children not to discuss around polite company. However, the extent to which limits are pushed depends largely on the media outlet. While television broadcasters and cable networks have to obey Federal Communication Commission laws on obscenity and indecency, print outlets and Web sites such as *The Onion* do not have such heavy restrictions. No matter in what media outlet the humor is showcased, I believe that calls for violence, bigotry, and xenophobia are less tolerated as humorous. For example, *The New Yorker* magazine learned that not all satire is perceived the same way. Recall its July 2008 cover of Barack Obama dressed as a Muslim and Michelle Obama dressed as a terrorist, with a photo of Osama bin Laden in the background and a burning American flag in the fireplace. [M]any people thought the satire went too far and reinforced stereotypes. . . . This example tells us that there are limits to certain groups' tolerance of satire.

Waisanen: Mark Katz, President Clinton's humor writer (yes, this was an official position!), said that in politics, you "can do jokes about the smoke and not the fire. We can do jokes about the hoopla of impeachment, but not what brought us to the brink of impeachment." I also once read *The Daily Show* correspondent Mo Rocca's comments that during the Iraq War, "Since we couldn't make fun of the events themselves, we could make fun of some of the coverage of the events." While perhaps not holding true in every situation, these comments generally tell us that there are serious limitations to humor itself—primarily that it's only one . . . mode of communicating among many other choices that might be made. Of course, any effort to curtail what is or is not appropriate in comic discourses should also be seen as suspect, as comedians are some of our best critics and free speech advocates, providing alternative interpretations and attitudes about public events when sorely needed.

Heather LaMarre: One of the comedian's roles is to test limits. And right now we have that going on with Colbert's SuperPAC, this would be a perfect example of limit testing. Never before can I think of that, in a time when a piece of satire was taken outside the comedic . . . form. And he has now created satirical PSAs, he's raising real money, real people are actually contributing their real dollars to this satirical SuperPAC. . . . [Colbert is] forcing the media to pay attention because he's moving outside his late-night show.

Williams: For all its faults, the rules of professional journalism are very explicit. . . . It is a profession, people are trained how to do it. . . . When we get to comedy as an increasingly influential way in which citizens understand the political world, then . . . I get a little queasy, because I think the rules are *very* unclear about what someone like Jon Stewart is doing and what he's not doing . . . I don't think we have a good way of thinking about "What is their responsibility? What is it okay to talk about and how is it okay to talk about it?"

Has humor always played a key role in politics?

Holbert: There is a long history of political leaders calling for satirists to be jailed, excommunicated, or censored. . . . I would argue that the jury is still out on the degree and nature of satire's influence. There is much more work to be done at a wide range of levels of analysis before we can offer any valid or reliable conclusions in relation to this empirical question.

Dannagal Young: Humor has always played an important role in political life. In fact, satirists like Aristophanes writing in ancient Greece used rich political satire and irony to expose hypocrisy and flaws among elites and within policies and institutions. What we see now is a media environment in which the former division between entertainment and information has become obsolete, hence we tend to think of political humor as a "new" thing. . . . In reality, humor has always had a very natural place in politics, particularly in democratic regimes where elected officials are accountable for their actions and citizens look at them with a critical eye.

Waisanen: Humor has probably played a role in just about every election and political circumstance. While we can look back to ancient figures such as Cicero for advice on how wit can be used in the political realm, I would argue humor's centrality to the political process has less to do with politics and more to do with how humor is found in every human society. What might be found humorous in one society or culture often differs from another, but I think one would be hard-pressed to find a situation where humor was not involved to some extent. Even when humor is not a part of "official" public discourse, humor is a regular part of group communication and is thus as much a part of "unofficial" interpersonal communication and backroom, informal political conversations as anything else.

Williams: I think that humor has always played a part in American elections and politics, but we notice it more at some points than others. . . . [I]f you go back to the earliest days of the American republic . . . a lot of the campaign arguments were made in political cartoons. I show my class cartoons that were aimed at Thomas Jefferson, that pointed to his supposed loyalty to France, um, you know, there were no mentions of "freedom fries" at that point, but, the idea that he was more loyal to France was brought out in cartoons. There were allusions to his relationship with Sally Hemings in the newspapers of the time; there was the kind of, you know, satirical character assassination that we take for granted today. Also, if you think about the late nineteenth century and the political cartoons of Thomas Nast . . . they were effective in reaching the audience he wanted.

What are the effects of humorous media?

Holbert: Political satire programming attracts a highly knowledgeable audience (you need to know a thing or two about politics if you are going to get the jokes), so does political satire generate humor or are those individuals who are already knowledgeable about politics selectively exposing themselves to this material? It is most likely a bit of both.

As for attitudes and behaviors, there is no question . . . political entertainment media can impact an audience member's attitudes. . . . However, questions still remain concerning how long lasting these effects are, how well they stand up to counterpersuasion, and whether insights generated from satire can impact how other pieces of political information (e.g., from news) are processed cognitively. On the behavioral front, there has been work done on how political entertainment media exposure can generate political discussion. Someone sees something funny about a political topic and then discusses it with others, or a piece of political humor is not fully understood by an audience member and they talk to friends or family members about it in order to gain some clarification about the message's meaning.

Landreville: [C]onflicting findings . . . suggest that political humor and satire are much more nuanced than researchers once believed. Humor and satire can be complicated messages that demand quite a bit of cognitive energy for people to decode, or humor and satire can be fairly simple messages that people disregard and do not pay much attention to. Both ways of processing these messages (critically and uncritically) can lead to different effects. . . . Thus, it is very difficult to summarize the effects of such a diverse and complicated genre. However, there have been links [found between] late-night comedy viewing to increased presidential debate viewing for young people ... [and] to increased traditional media use for political information. These studies are evidence for a democratizing effect of late-night comedy. Other studies have found increased cynicism for politicians after exposure to late-night comedy and a lack of information acquisition and memory. ... It's complicated.

Young: Literature to date has demonstrated nuanced effects of political humor. ... For instance, exposure to political humor programming, particularly among those people who are not politically engaged, can spark an interest and attention to politics, leading to information seeking. ... In addition, political humor has been found to increase the "salience" of issues and concepts that rest at the heart of political jokes. This means that people who frequently watch late-night comedy jokes about a political candidate for being boring, unintelligent, or dishonest will be more likely to have that trait come to mind when they think of that particular candidate in the future. We know that people who report watching shows like *The Daily Show* are more politically interested in general, more politically knowledgeable, more participatory in political life, and more likely to discuss politics with friends and family than people who do not watch such programming. While these are merely correlational findings, they do suggest that there is a unique audience of young, politically savvy people who are tuning into these shows.

In terms of the subtle cognitive implications of political humor, one of the reasons that political humor has received so much attention from scholars [is that] humor seems to hold a certain persuasive capacity that other forms of discourse do not. Recent work has . . . [found] that humor is actually less likely to foster the kind of "counterargumentation" or "argument scrutiny" that serious discourse usually receives. . . . People just do not scrutinize arguments received through humor to the extent that they do when [it's] presented seriously.

LaMarre: It's long been thought that the effect was limited because people used it in a cathartic way: They laughed at the comedian and then they went home and went about their business. And it's only in, probably since the 1980s, that we started doing effects research, looking at what happens after they leave the play or they leave the stand-up comedy club or they turn the TV off and go about their daily lives.

In that area, we are starting to understand a couple of basic things. One is message receptivity. People have their guard down . . . so they're more open and receptive to messages [than] maybe otherwise . . . [humor] sort of disarms them . . . There's a gateway hypothesis . . . that entertainment brings in the "politically uninterested"— especially young people, and that leads to more information seeking, participatory behavior, voting.

Williams: First, I think that, I think that *The Daily Show* and *The Colbert Report,* for their audience, do the same thing that the nightly network news broadcasts used to do. . . . *The Daily Show* . . . provides, in thirty minutes . . . a way of thinking about what's happened [and] the media that delivered that information to you. And how are you going to do that in a way where people can just change the channel any time they want?

Well, I think humor is a real . . . a very effective way of doing that. . . . [W]e trust Jon Stewart, just like we trusted Walter Cronkite, and I think that part of that trust for Jon Stewart is the idea that you know who he is. You know that he is gonna make fun of things, but he's not gonna make stuff up. That he's going to be scrupulous about the kind of facts that he introduces. . . . I think we're gonna see what happens. We're gonna see where the youth vote goes. We're gonna see whether new media mobilizes people [and how it's] gonna affect mobilization and participation [over] the next couple of elections.

Does humor help people engage in politics or create apathy toward the process?

Holbert: Researchers who are critical of various types of political entertainment argue that it makes a skeptical citizenry (i.e., a democratic good) into a cynical citizenry (i.e., a democratic evil). There is some empirical evidence to support this claim, but it is also the case that those who are more cynical about politics naturally gravitate to this material as well (once again, an issue of selective exposure). With this being stated, there are a host of potentially positive effects that have been linked to various types of political entertainment media outlets. Empirical studies have shown that certain political entertainment messages can generate critical thinking on political issues, create greater breadth and depth of attitudinal structures, and (at least indirectly) increase political behaviors like giving money to political causes, talking about politics, or watching political debates.

LaMarre: We've answered the question of whether it engages audiences, we know that. But engages them how and to what end? We're not sure. In some cases, we find they learn more about the issues. In other cases, we find they don't understand the sarcasm or satire, and so they come away misinformed. In a lot of cases, we find evidence that, because comedians . . . cherry-pick segments and then use them to an exaggerated point to make it funny, sometimes audiences don't understand that it *was* exaggerated.

Is political humor just for liberals?

Landreville: Political humor and especially satire is about deconstructing politics, politicians, policy, institutions, and authority. This deconstruction often involves questioning, mocking, and criticizing the status quo, the traditions, and the standards. From mocking a politician's expensive haircut to mocking the hypocritical politician who employs illegal residents yet rails against immigration, humorists are making statements about society. Perhaps liberals are more attracted to satire and humor that exposes the hypocrisy of traditions and traditional society because part of being liberal is being progressive and deconstructive of restrictive societal norms. However, conservatives are certainly attracted to satire and humor that exposes the hypocrisy of liberalism and progressive society. That is probably why some conservatives watch *The Daily Show* and *The Colbert Report* and view it as interesting and insightful comedy on liberals—these shows do not hold back on criticizing anyone. In the end, I think all shades of political red, blue, and purple benefit from political humor.

Waisanen: This issue is far more complicated than it might appear. Certainly, comedians like Jon Stewart have tended to embrace a leftist political perspective, while in recent years, others like Dennis Miller have leveraged their comic credentials toward conservative political causes. . . . But I think a more important consideration is to move beyond thinking about this issue in terms of people or political worldviews, asking instead what kind of radical or conservative perspective might be invited by any particular *act* of political humor. That is, how much does any comic act, like a particular joke, invite its audiences to think of their worlds in ways that maintain or interrogate the status quo? In a single HBO stand-up special by someone like Chris Rock, for example, I think we can note ways that some jokes both embrace and perpetuate racial and ethnic stereotypes as much as other jokes invite us to think critically about them. As such, the politics of comedy is probably best described and evaluated as close to each text and context as possible.

Finally, what happens when politicians try to be funny?

Holbert: It depends on the type of humor. There are certain politicians who have comedic timing. President Obama is one . . . former governor Mike Huckabee of Arkansas is another recent politico who comes to mind . . . When they have [comedic skill], they can use it to connect to an audience. However, if the presentation of humorous material appears forced, then, just as at dinner parties, people seek other company really quick.

A special case of humor often used by politicians is self-deprecation. Senator John McCain is a classic example of someone who uses self-deprecation well [as was] Vice President Albert Gore, Jr. in the latter years of the Clinton presidency. . . . Politicians as elites are always looking for ways to appear more common, and self-deprecation is one way to go about achieving this goal. However, . . . self-deprecation is effective only when the focus of the deprecation is perceived to be a true personal weakness/character flaw. For example, former president Bill Clinton may make fun of his famous temper, [but] if the politician pokes fun at a personal characteristic that many perceive to be an actual positive trait, then the act of self-deprecation could be seen by many as a tawdry attempt to receive praise. Such acts of praise seeking are never well received by the general public.

Self-deprecation can also be used for image repair. A recent example would be Governor Rick Perry, who ran a series of television advertisements leading up to the Iowa caucuses where he poked fun at himself for not being the best debater . . . the most effective strategic communication decision his campaign could make was to acknowledge the personal weakness and make light of it in some way in these advertisements.

Landreville: It is risky business. When politicians attempt to correct a perceived failure, such as Rick Perry's "oops" moment in a Republican presidential debate, and use humor to do so . . . they could be making themselves more down-to-earth and carefree, but they could also be bringing more attention to a negative event. . . . Also, if the attempt at humor is awkward and uncomfortable, then the politician will be portrayed as stiff, unlikeable, and elitist. Clearly, playing with humor is like playing with fire for politicians.

Waisanen: To an extent, humor always both unites and divides audiences. When politicians try to be funny, they can unite one audience while dividing another. Ronald

Reagan was known for his humor, but it's easy to see how a quip like "The nine most terrifying words in the English language are: 'I'm from the government and I'm here to help'" could reinforce one audience's belief that the government was a problem, as much as it confirmed for another that the president's beliefs were a problem. Some humor can unite more than divide, but in so doing, may run the risk of losing its critical edge. Think Jay Leno versus Jon Stewart. Leno plays his humor relatively safe and maintains a mainstream, large audience, while Stewart plays to a smaller cable audience with humor that is more divisive and critical. This is the tough tightrope that politicians themselves walk when attempting to use humor.

Williams: [W]ho was it who has on their tombstone something like "Dying is easy, comedy is hard"? Comedy is really hard. And some people can do it, and some people can't . . . you have to have a certain amount of being relaxed enough and comfortable in—at least seeming to be comfortable in—your own skin to make jokes. . . . [O]ne of the ways that comedy can often help politicians [is in] humaniz[ing] them. Nixon, as uncomfortable as he looked saying "Sock it to me!" there was something about his willingness to do that.

[O]ften, when it comes to celebrity—and politicians are celebrities—we have this desire to get to know who they *really* are, as if we can kind of puncture somehow the public image that they show us. And often, humor is used or seems to be a way to get past that public mask.

LaMarre: I think it depends on when you use it and do it. President Obama sent Betty White a Happy Birthday message [recently], and he cracked a joke about wanting to see her birth certificate. And I, myself, found that hysterical! . . . Even the leader of the free world can tell a joke. I think the big question is going to be . . . whether people under thirty are . . . developing a sense of humor about politics that's good for democracy or a disgust about politics that's bad for democracy. That remains to be seen!

PARTICIPANT PROFILES

R. Lance Holbert is in the The Ohio State University's School of Communications. He is the author (with Maxwell McCombs, Spiro Kiousus, and Wayne Wanta) of *The News & Public Opinion: Media Effects on the Elements of Civic Life* (2011, Polity).

Heather LaMarre is in the department of strategic communications at Temple University. She studies how and why social and entertainment media are changing public relations, politics, and news.

Kristen Landreville is in the department of communication and journalism at the University of Wyoming. She studies the intersection of mass and interpersonal communication on political and social outcomes.

Don Waisanen is in the Baruch College School of Public Affairs. Before entering academia, he worked in broadcast journalism and as a political speechwriter. He is a contributor to the TSP Community Page ThickCulture.

Bruce Williams is in media studies at the University of Virginia. He is the author (with Michael Delli Carpini) of *After Broadcast News: Media Regimes. Democracy, and the New Information Environment* (2012, Cambridge University Press).

Dannagal Young is in the communications department at the University of Delaware. She is the founder of Breaking Boundaries, an online forum for the interdisciplinary study of politics and entertainment.

TSP tie-in

collective action frames

I f you have participated in a march or a demonstration, or have even signed a petition on Facebook, you have participated in collective action. When collective action becomes organized, purposeful, and institutionalized, it is considered a social movement.

Participants in social movements and other forms of collective action often create and draw upon what sociologists have termed *collective action frames*. Collective action frames are lenses through which social phenomena are interpreted. They offer a way to categorize and understand the world; in essence, they are ways to make sense of our experiences. Frames are actively constructed and can be contentious, because they are often created in opposition to existing frames.

These frames are important because social movements rely on frames to legitimate their claims and mobilize actions. Sociologists David Snow and Robert Benford have categorized the core framing tasks—that is, the types of framing a movement needs to do in order to give its cause meaning and legitimacy—as *diagnostic framing*, which identifies problems and assigns blame; *prognostic framing*, which proposes solutions; and *motivational framing*, which provides a rationale for engagement and is, essentially, a call for action. For example, if a social movement was fighting the presence of a waste incinerator to be located in a poor neighborhood, the activists may decide to frame the presence of the incinerator as an environmental injustice and blame city officials or the company that owns the incinerator (diagnostic framing). The group might also suggest that the incinerator be removed from the neighborhood and that residents be given more power in deciding what hazards would be allowed in their neighborhood in the future (prognostic framing). Finally, the group might rally around a cry for environmental justice and equal treatment (motivational framing).

Once frames are constructed, there are frequently struggles over the frames. In simpler terms, these are struggles over meaning. For example, one Sociological Images post shows an Occupy Wall Street movement flyer that attempted to frame the group's actions as serious protest, not just "camping," as detractors had described their large-scale sit-ins. Instead, the flyer shows, the protestors are doing hard work, "Petitioning Government for Redress of Grievances." As you can see in the piece, written by Lisa Wade, the Occupy Phoenix group's flyer illustrates the power of language and the struggle to control it.

Social movements aren't the only actors that frame issues. For example, the media also engages in framing of issues, sometimes in direct opposition to existing frames. On The Society Pages, you can read a roundtable on the media framing of the Trayvon Martin murder that dissects the many approaches taken in reporting. Whether media outlets chose to focus on the importance of self-protection and "standing your ground," as the shooter said he was doing when he killed Martin, on the many community gatherings and responses to the murder, or on the race, age, or motivations of Martin vividly illustrates the importance of creating and controlling meaning. One sociologist included in the roundtable even pointed out how protestors trying to raise awareness of the injustice they saw in police response to Martin's murder had been carrying signs and wearing hoodies, proclaiming, "I am Trayvon Martin." Perhaps, the scholar said, their signs should have read, "I am George Zimmerman"—that alternate framing, acknowledging privilege and the racial dimensions of the case, she thought, would change the conversation drastically.

Browse to thesocietypages.org/politics for links to content about framing and social movements from throughout our collection.

HOLLIE NYSETH BREHM

critical takes

the paradoxes of black republicans

COREY FIELDS

n the run-up to the 2012 presidential election, Stacey Dash—eternally youthful actress and star of the '90s classic *Clueless*—tweeted, "Vote for Mitt Romney. The only choice for your future." The blowback, in true Twitter form, came quickly and not so nicely. I'll spare you the most venomous responses. But a central theme was captured by a tweet from Tretista Kelverian, who joked, "You're an unemployed black woman endorsing @MittRomney. You're voting against yourself thrice. You poor beautiful idiot." The sentiment behind this biting response—that black interests and Republican partisanship are fundamentally discordant—has come up in every conversation I had with an African American Republican, as well as every conversation I had with others *about* African American Republicans.

Black Republicans report feeling excluded from the African American political community, and their beliefs are often maligned as racially inauthentic. Some revel in their outsider status, provoking controversy with inflammatory statements about race and racism. Yet, for the vast majority, the charges sting. Accusations of racial betrayal hurt not only because they are insulting, but also because the "sellout" narrative fundamentally misrepresents black Republicans' political agenda. Further, obsessing over whether African American Republicans are sellouts obscures important differences *among* them, particularly in regard to how they think about race and social policies. Rather than focus on whether they are "black enough," political analysts would be better served by examining *how* race structures the politics of these conservatives. Once we move past the sellout question, it becomes clear that there are important racially motivated divides among African American Republicans.

Given the negative reputation associated with being an African American Republican, it is not surprising that there are not that many of them. After emancipation, the overwhelming majority of black Americans supported the Republican Party. However, since the 1930s, they have been steadily withdrawing their support from the Party of Lincoln. The 1968 election, in which Nixon deployed his infamous "Southern Strategy," garnered all-time low levels of Republican partisanship among blacks. That is, until the 2008 presidential election, when 96% of black voters cast their vote for Barack

Obama, the Democratic candidate. Polling before the 2012 election revealed this number wasn't likely to change.

This dramatic reversal of partisanship has left very few African Americans part of the coalition of Republican voters. Some estimates suggest only 3% of Republican voters are black: African American Republicans are rare among both black voters and Republican voters.

In spite of this rarity—or, perhaps, because of it—African American Republicans are enjoying their highest profile since the Reconstruction era. This attention extends beyond the usual big names like Condoleezza Rice, Colin Powell, and Clarence Thomas. For instance, Mia Love—the black, Mormon, small-town Utah mayor who's running for Congress—used a prime-time speaking spot to wow the audience at the Republican National Convention. Herman Cain ran a brief, high-profile campaign for the 2012 Republican presidential nomination. And the November 2010 midterm elections saw a record number of African American Republicans running for Congress: thirty-two candidates made bids for office and fourteen won their primaries. Only two, Allen West of Florida and Tim Scott of South Carolina, won in the general election (they became the first African American Republicans in Congress since 2003). Even pop music is in on the black Republican renaissance, with Nas and Jay Z's 2010 single "Black Republican."

For such a small group, African American Republicans are everywhere, but their foray into popular culture hasn't been a walk in the park. Alongside their white conservative counterparts, African American Republicans have gotten their share of mocking, but in their case, the humor is based on the very *idea* that a black person would be Republican.

Whether it results in attacking or mocking, most responses to African American Republicans are grounded in the idea that blackness is incompatible with the Grand Old Party. As a result, black conservatives are still seen as somehow "less black" because of their partisanship.

not just uncle toms

Given this context, it is surprising to find African American Republican activists expressing strong connections to other black people: they don't see themselves as "less black." They tell me they live in black neighborhoods, attend black churches, are members of black organizations, and work with black people. Their lives are subject to the same residential and workplace racial segregation that many African Americans experience. Unfailingly, interviewees refer to "us," "we," and "our community" when referencing black people. Far from being estranged from other blacks, the African American Republicans I talked to are deeply embedded in black communities.

Michael Dawson describes this feeling of connectedness as "linked fate," and his research suggests linked fate is a key driver of African American political behavior. All participants in my research, too, express pretty high levels of linked fate, but there are also important differences in how they engage in Republican politics. African American Republicans have varied feelings about their connection to other blacks: some value it, and others find it troublesome. The fact that all of the black Republicans I talked to felt connected, but did not attach the same meaning and importance to that connection, is key to delineating their political activities.

Based on my research, African American Republicans can actually be categorized into two groups based on the centrality of race in their worldview. I call the first "race-blind." They see racial status, and any associated discrimination, as marginal to the life experience of blacks. Instead, they believe personal choices and pathological values are responsible for racial disparities in the U.S. This is consistent with the "sellout" reputation that stigmatizes African American Republicans.

I believe the second group of black Republicans is characterized by a worldview of "racial uplift." While not denying a role for personal responsibility, they see blacks as constrained by blocked opportunities and racism—an American structural reality that affects the lives of all African Americans.

Unlike their raceblind counterparts, racial uplift African American Republicans place race at the *center* of their political outlook.

Both raceblind and racial uplift African American Republicans see the GOP's policy program as the best way to meet the needs of black communities, but they define those needs in contradicting ways. Thus, variations in the perceived importance of race structure ideas about black interests and impact African Americans' expressions of Republican partisanship. In terms of actual policy preferences, there is actually not that much difference between the two types of African American Republicans. They all support similar social and fiscal policies. They simply invoke different rhetorical strategies in support of those preferences.

raceblind vs. racial uplift

Consistent with other accounts of raceblind politics, African American Republicans who can be categorized as raceblind de-emphasize the importance of race in both the causes and solutions to problems facing the black community. They work to eliminate race from their policy consideration, going so far as to suggest that racially conscious social policies are no different than Jim Crow, because both acknowledge and promote a racial distinction. For them,

Republican policies are ideologically and philosophically appealing. In contrast, the racial uplift African American Republicans present social policies in light of how they affect black people. For African American Republicans who employ this framing, the appeal of traditional GOP policy positions is not tied to an abstract, ideological notion of being "right." Rather, these policies are appealing because they are best suited to place black people on the path to middle-class success. These differences are quite stark when African American Republicans talk about specific policies.

Kevin,* like all the subjects in my study, is primarily active in state and local Republican politics. He's an entrepreneur living outside of Atlanta, and he came to Republican politics to escape what he described as the "tiring" politics of the Democratic Party. "I just got so tired of constantly hearing the same things, but not getting any results," he explained over coffee. "I guess I just feel like we, as black people, have to stop seeing everything in black and white. You find what you want to see. You keep looking for racism and you'll find it soon enough. I just try to do my own thing and let my success speak for itself." Accordingly, he values conservative economic policies based on "principles that benefit everybody," not just narrow interest groups. His pet issue is "tax reform,"

---

* All respondent names are pseudonyms.

in particular repealing the inheritance tax. This tax seemed a strange canard, given that Kevin and his heirs were unlikely to ever be subject to it. But Kevin insisted it's an issue of fairness and an ideological commitment to keeping the state out of his wallet. "What it [tax reform] does is keep us from the death tax [inheritance tax] . . . that keeps us from being able to transfer to our children stuff that we want to pass down to them . . . I think it's a money issue, period. And people try to make it into a black issue, and it's actually a class warfare issue between the haves and the have-nots." Consistent with this raceblind approach, Kevin sees low taxes and pro-business policies from a race-neutral, ideological perspective. When he does invoke social categories, he draws on class. In his mind, fiscally conservative policies are good for everyone.

Jason sees the benefit of low taxes differently. In our conversations, he recalled growing up in close proximity to economic deprivation. Although he never lived in what he labels the "ghetto neighborhood," he rode the bus with kids from that neighborhood. He believes such black neighborhoods suffer from a lack of investment. "Look around. You don't see no businesses. No kind of economic development." When Jason echoes the broader Republican call for lower taxes, he frames that support in racial uplift terms that stress the relevance of low taxes for black people. "When taxes are lower there is more money to invest back into the community. How can you support black businesses if you're losing half of your paycheck to taxes?"

Steven, another racial uplift African American Republican, draws on similar rhetoric when discussing the benefits of conservative fiscal policies: "When taxes are low, that encourages business development and entrepreneurship in black communities. When taxes are lower, there is more money to encourage business. And that's what we need in our communities. All these empty storefronts could be filled with black-owned companies. Black folks think high taxes are good for social programs, but we're really shooting ourselves in the foot because it doesn't encourage black businesses." Steven goes so far as to juxtapose low taxes against social welfare programs; in his calculation, lower taxes will ultimately provide the more resources for black communities. For Jason, Steven, and their counterparts, lower taxes mean blacks will have more money to invest in their communities.

The raceblind/racial uplift framing tension goes beyond taxes, of course. Although support for school vouchers was almost universal among the African American Republicans I interviewed, some saw vouchers as an expression of the power of markets while others saw vouchers as giving parents control over their children's education. Bobby deploys a raceblind framing that draws on the power of market-based reform as he describes his support for vouchers: they "force schools to compete. Once you give people choices and schools can't count on that money, they'll get their acts together or they'll close." Samuel sees vouchers through the lens of race. "You know why I love school vouchers? Because they give black parents control over their kids' schools. It puts black parents in charge of black kids. Not some white person from the school board who doesn't have any idea of what black children in black communities need."

With these distinct framings of Republican policy, it would be easy to envision raceblind African American Republicans as callow, self-serving Uncle Toms and racial uplift African American Republicans as quasi-Black Nationalists down for revolution. But it would be careless to caricature raceblind African American Republicans as delusional stooges, and it would misrepresent racial uplift partisans to suggest they're champions of social justice, calling for the overthrow of a racist social order. Even the staunchest of raceblind African American Republicans will agree that there are racist individuals and racism exists—they just don't see much effectiveness in launching race-based political appeals. Ignoring race is seen as the best route to ensure that blacks are assimilated into mainstream American culture. And, though racial uplift African American Republicans see structural racism as a key problem facing blacks, their call to action is centered on the idea that blacks have to be responsible, individually and collectively, for their own success. This does little to call into question the institutional forces that produce racial inequality, but retains hope for an environment in which blacks can get in on the fun happening at the top of the pyramid.

rethinking african american republicans

Whether we see them speaking to packed stadiums at nominating conventions or on cable news pugnaciously attacking the "poverty pimps" of the Democratic Party, the picture the media paints of African American Republicans suggests they are unified in their rejection of identity politics. However, the raceblind antics of politicians like Mia Love and Herman Cain don't tell the full story of African American Republicans. Attending to how race orients their political beliefs illuminates an important difference among African American Republicans. For raceblind African American Republicans, connection to racial identity is deep and often invoked as motivation for their partisanship, but race is deemphasized in the arena of social policy. In contrast, racial uplift African American Republicans see everything through the lens of race, but deploy their racialized worldviews in support of conservative social policy. While there is consistent support for Republican policy positions across the core of black conservatives, the motivations and justifications for those positions vary in important ways, but we can only see them when we move past trying to determine whether Republican politics and the people who engage in them can be authentically black.

In many ways, the charges of "sellout" or "Uncle Tom" reflect the anxieties of other political actors rather than the motivations of African American Republicans. So while most conversations about African American Republicans start by asking some variant of the "Are they black enough?" question, a more useful question might be "What meaning do they attach to being black?" This draws attention to the processes through which race and racial identity can be marshaled in support of a broad range of political ideologies and social policies, though this analytic shift requires an agnostic approach to any specific policy issues. In the case of African American Republicans, that means I must refrain from adjudicating the "rightness" or "wrongness" of their policy preferences. Such judgments are well beyond the scope of my research, but, more importantly, they shed little light on the processes through which race gets linked to political behavior.

So, once we've stopped assuming race as the "cause" of certain political behavior, we can begin to ask more expansive questions. For instance, raceblind African American Republicans enjoy much more success within the Republican Party than their racial uplift counterparts. Why? Additionally, among black conservatives, the same "levels" of racial identity can produce very different political behaviors. This suggests that a broad range of political actions can be done in the name of "black people" and demands that we direct attention to how and why racial identity—or *any* identity, for that matter—is brought to bear on political decisions. Time spent on considering "racial authenticity" is time that would be better spent in taking on these more analytically useful questions.

Race, this is to say, is not a static category with self-evident meanings. We cannot assume the meaning of race to be consistent and constant. Indeed, recent research demonstrates that African Americans and other racial minorities vary in the extent to which their racial identities are meaningful across a range of social domains. A similar trend seems to be true in the political arena. By showing differences in the way that race structures policy framings among African American Republicans, my research urges the undertaking of questions about when and why race matters in political behavior and how racial identity gets linked to a particular political program. The relative rarity of black Republicans cannot be allowed to undermine true inquiry or excuse monolithic representations of them as somehow both unique and uniform.

RECOMMENDED READING

Michael Dawson. 1995. *Behind the Mule: Race and Class in African American Politics*, Princeton, NJ: Princeton University Press. Shows how, despite increasing class diversity, race is still the dominant driver of African American political behavior. Introduces the concept of "linked fate" to account for African American political unity.

Angela Dillard. 2002. *Guess Who's Coming to Dinner Now: Multicultural Conservatism in America*, New York: New York University Press. Focuses on the intellectual leaders of various "minority" conservative factions and offers a comparative analysis of the motivations and philosophies of conservatives that cut across race, gender, and sexuality.

J. G. Conti, Stan Faryna, and Brad Stetson (editors). 1997. *Black and Right*, Westport, CT: Praeger. This collection of essays offers personal and political portraits of black conservatives in America.

Michael K. Fountroy. 2006. *Republicans and the Black Vote*, Boulder, CO: Lynne Rienner Publishers. Provides an overview of the history of African American participation in the Republican Party.

Christopher Allen Bracey. 2008. *Saviors or Sellouts: The Promise and Perils of Black Conservatism, from Booker T. Washington to Condoleezza Rice*, Boston, MA: Beacon. Examines black neo-conservative thinkers and politicians to explain why conservatism remains a coherent ideological alternative for African Americans today.

let herman be herman: republican presidential candidate herman cain and the utility of blackness for the political right

ENID LOGAN

{ 11

n November of 2011, Herman Cain was the front-runner for the Republican presidential nomination, embroiled in a sexual harassment scandal, and the darling of the Tea Party. There were widespread claims at that time that Cain's candidacy "proved" the far right was not racist. Like the 2007–2008 arguments that Barack Obama's ascent "proved" that the U.S. was now a "colorblind" nation, this claim was false and misleading.

In my 2011 book, *"At This Defining Moment": Barack Obama's Presidential Candidacy and the New Politics of Race*, I focused on contemporary racial politics among those on the left of the political spectrum. The Cain phenomenon, how-ever, allows for an exploration of the emergent dimensions of the racial politics of the right—in particular, the political utility of blackness for conservatives in the present age.

To contextualize the issues raised by Cain's campaign, it is useful to first consider how race played out for Obama in 2007–2008. I argue that Obama did not run a "raceless" pres-idential campaign, he did not "transcend" race, and he was elected not in *spite* of his race but in significant measure *because* of it.

In fact, race was used as a sort of oppositional frame. Obama was highly praised for the degree to which he was not a "traditional" black public figure, like Jesse Jackson, Al Sharpton, or other blacks with whom the wider (white) public had grown increasingly impatient. The candidate also won major points for his willingness to repudiate the supposed lifestyles and choices of the black poor. Consider his repeated calls for "Cousin Ray Ray," "Uncle Pookie," and other mythi-cal poor black men to "get up off the couch," "pull up their pants," and take "personal responsibility" for their own lives.

As a postracial black candidate, Obama was believed *through* his magical blackness to be able to reconcile Ameri-cans of all colors and creeds, grant whites absolution for the racial sins of the past, and redeem the nation by demonstrat-ing the U.S. to be again a place of open opportunity and tolerance. Obama was affable, charismatic, nonconfrontational, and highly articulate. In him, the pundits claimed, there was a man who would take the country beyond the "stale and tired" racial politics of the past. Firmly "rooted" in the black community, Obama was nevertheless not "limited to it" or "defined by it." Thus, we heard again and again, his ascent heralded the dawn of a "new politics of race."

In the 2012 presidential race, we were faced with a new set of questions raised by the candidacy of Herman Cain. In his run, race played out in some ways quite differently than it did for Obama, but there were striking parallels as well. What explains Cain's popularity on the right, and how was it tied to his race? When, and in what ways, did Cain seek to use race to his advantage (say, by reminding supporters of his blackness or claiming to be a victim of liberal racism), and when did he seek to de-emphasize it? What did Cain's staunch support among Tea Party types tell us about the racial politics of the most conservative Americans?

As we watched the campaign unfold, the answers to these questions were never entirely clear—in part because Herman Cain had been on the national radar for a relatively short time, and in part because his campaign underwent a number of surprising twists and turns in its brief existence.

The first of these was how Cain rocketed to the front of the GOP presidential pack, seemingly out of nowhere. We first heard of Herman Cain in the weeks following the Iowa straw poll, when many assumed that the field of serious contenders for the Republican presidential nomination had been largely established. But the former Godfather's Pizza CEO soon eclipsed the presumptive nominee, former Massachusetts governor Mitt Romney, and remained at the top of the polls for weeks.

The second major development in Cain's story was the emergence of reports of a series of unwelcome sexual advances the candidate allegedly made toward female employees as head of the National Restaurant Association. As with the first arc of his candidacy, the sexual assault scandal took on highly racialized dimensions: those on the right claimed that Cain had either been subject to a "high-tech lynching" by the liberal media or that the "Democrat machine" was trying to take him down. There was also the glaring, but largely unremarked-upon fact that all of the women who claimed Cain had sexually harassed them were white—*blond*, at that.

Cain managed to survive the scandal for several weeks. He vigorously denied the charges levied against him in unequivocal statements such as "No, there was no kind of settlement ever," "I have never met that woman in my life," and "I have never done anything inappropriate to anyone, ever, period!" As information contradicting Cain's statements began to materialize, the candidate lost both credibility and viability in the eyes of many political observers. But Cain's hard-core supporters rose to his defense, pouring money into his campaign coffers and booing moderators who raised questions about the harassment charges at the GOP presidential debate in Michigan.

You may remember that Cain eventually bowed out of the race, after an Atlanta woman named Ginger White came forward alleging that the two of them had had a thirteen year affair. Though Cain vigorously denied it, his brief, wacky, and somewhat farcical run for the White House was over. Still, it merits serious consideration, as related to the issues of race, blackness, and conservative electoral politics.

In an interview I did with a local television news station in October 2011, I was asked whether I thought Cain could win a significant proportion of the black vote. (Cain had claimed that at least a third of all black voters would turn out for him.) This question struck me as odd; it was clear then that Cain wasn't even seriously trying to court black voters. Many of the statements Cain made about blacks were insulting and belittling. He described African Americans as "brainwashed" by the Democratic Party, living on the "Democratic plantation." He implied that black voters lacked political intelligence and were unable to think for themselves. In one televised speech, Cain even said that since *he* had fully achieved the American dream, there was nothing (for African Americans) "to complain about!"

Other nonwhites and non-Christians were dismissed as quickly. Candidate Cain stated in March of last year that, if he were to become president, he would not appoint a Muslim to his cabinet or to a federal judgeship. As he told the magazine *Christianity Today*, "[B]ased upon the little knowledge that I have of the Muslim religion, you know, they have an objective to convert all infidels or kill them." In October 2011, riding high in the polls, he called for an electrified, twenty-foot fence along the U.S. border with Mexico, surrounded by signs declaring in English and in Spanish, "It will kill you." The same month, in an interview with a conservative talk radio station, Cain said many blacks on the left were more racist than the white conservatives they complained about—a claim that strongly echoes the frequent complaints of "reverse racism" we hear from the right.

Overall, therefore, it appears Herman Cain's chief utility for the right was to attack or further delegitimize the collective interests of blacks and other nonwhites in the twenty-first century. In a way, Cain's candidacy was a kind of preparatory response to the coming demographic tidal wave. By the year 2050, whites will slip to less than half of the population for the first time in the nation's history, and the United States will become a "majority-minority" nation. But

Cain's candidacy represented a very partial and cynical response to this change. Rather than representing an honest attempt to make conservativism a more diverse and inclusive political movement, it came across as a push back; part of a larger, Tea Party-led attempt to keep power, wealth, and national identity in the control of whites, even as they lose grasp of the reins.

I concede that black conservativism is potentially a legitimate strain of black political thought. But the face of black conservatism we see most often today is not about or for black people, but about and for white people (consider for example, Larry Elder, Alan Keyes, Allen West, Michael S. Steele, Walter Williams, Juan Williams, and Artur Davis, to name a few). I suggest that much of Herman Cain's appeal stemmed from the fact that he was willing to speak the kinds of "truths" about race that whites on the far right are clamoring to hear in an age in which they feel imperiled. It also explains polemical right-winger Ann Coulter's declaration "our blacks are better than theirs."

It is crucial to point out, however, that Barack Obama performed the same function for white Democrats in 2007–2008. During his campaign, candidate Obama spoke the "truths" about race that white *liberals* most wanted to hear: that they were good and noble people, that they were absolved of the sins of the past, that racism in the United States was largely vanquished, and that Jackson, Sharpton, and poor blacks as a whole were in fact highly problematic people.

Some of the racial "truths," then, that Cain spoke during his run were quite similar to those spoken by Obama, just put more bluntly. Cain, too, stood against "quota-style" affirmative action, called for black personal responsibility ("What's there to complain about?" "If you don't have a job, it's your fault," etc.), and, with his "brainwashed" statement, questioned the common sense, judgment, and worldview of most black Americans. This rhetorical tie is no mere coincidence. As I argue in my book, the convergence between conservative and liberal stances on racial matters is an indication of the degree to which American racial politics as a whole have shifted to the right in the last several decades. As a number of scholars of race have written, where affirmative action, welfare rights, school desegregation, and the enforcement of antidiscrimination law were once cornerstones of liberalism, such initiatives are now only meekly defended, if at all.

It is also important to consider Cain's "performance of blackness." I claim in my book that Obama's bounded, depoliticized performances of blackness (affectionate fist-bumps with Michelle, demonstrated serious basketball habit, ability to slip in and out of "black" forms of speech, and occasional references to elements of hip-hop culture) were highly appealing to many whites, as it seemed that they might serve as the basis for a revitalized, newly authentic American national identity.

Cain's "performances" of blackness, however, were somewhat different. He said that if he were the "flavor of the month" he must be "black walnut," joked that his Secret Service code name should be "Cornbread," and began the speech in which he officially declared his candidacy in front of a nearly all-white, majority Tea Party audience by saying, "Aww, shucky ducky now." A number of writers have characterized this as a kind of "minstrelsy," describing Cain in these episodes as self-deprecating, bowing and stooping before whites. The most well-known example came from the journalist Touré, who literally referred to Cain as a minstrel in an article in *Time* magazine, then later on MSNBC.

While I think there is *something* to this reading, the idea that he merely made himself a racial "act" doesn't seem fully logical to me. Cain is extraordinarily self-confident, often bordering on arrogant (after all, he refers to himself in the third person). His Tea Party base was looking to him not as a sidekick but as the leader of the nation. Instead, Cain seemed to be saying that it is not necessary to take black people or blackness itself seriously. He demonstrated that it was okay, or even humorous, for conservatives to articulate age-old stereotypes about blacks or even to make references to slavery (e.g., "the Democratic political plantation") to defend their points of view against those of prominent blacks and liberals in general.

Defending Herman Cain was, in part, a means of crying "reverse racism" out loud. It was also an attempt to forcefully deny that the conservative movement remains a white, old boys' club in which people (i.e., men) of color might occasionally function as charming adornments. Cain's staunchest supporters were found among those who sought to "take America back"—back from Barack Obama, back from "socialism," back from secular liberalism, gays and lesbians, the Occupy Wall Street movement, and outspoken, progressive leaders of color—in short, back to the good old days when white hegemony was absolute, since today it is in inevitable decline.

12

the perils of
transcendence

ANDRA GILLESPIE

n the weeks after Newark, New Jersey's Democratic mayor
Cory Booker admitted he found the early attack ads of this
general election cycle to be "nauseating" and that, in implicit
contrast to President Obama, he saw the public benefits of
private equity firms like Bain Capital, his comments were
used as a Republican fund-raising tool and excoriated by liberal critics. While many analysts have focused on the effi-
cacy of Obama's Bain Capital offensive or debated the merits
of surrogates openly critiquing the candidates they support,
it is important to also consider the advantages and disadvantages of being a politician who brands himself as politically
transcendent.

When we refer to political transcendence in the American
context, we often mean racial transcendence, particularly
the ability of minority candidates to appeal to voters beyond
their racial or ethnic community. Scholars have been debating

the utility of racially transcendent political campaigns since the 1970s, when political scientist Charles Hamilton urged Democratic candidates to deracialize their campaign platforms. Hamilton was concerned that white voters would defect to the Republican Party because they found the racial rhetoric of the Democratic Party to be too heavy-handed. By casting a progressive platform in racially transcendent terms, he argued that Democrats would be able to unite a rainbow coalition around issues that would benefit everyone, including blacks.

Booker himself gained national prominence as part of a fresh, young cohort of African American politicians who put their own spin on deracialization. They have been unafraid to challenge the orthodoxy of the civil rights establishment that dominated black electoral politics for a generation. Their embrace of pragmatic, market-based remedies for social inequality and their rhetorical de-emphasis of racial issues have a special appeal beyond the African American community, in which many had grown weary of perceived stridency of activists and elected officials who wore their racial politics on their sleeves.

Much of the scholarly work on deracialization has focused on the impact of such deracialized campaigns on voter behavior or whether deracialized politicians proved to be more effective officeholders. While this has certainly been a worthwhile path of inquiry, there are other important facets to study. Young, deracialized black politicians often seek to be postpartisan in addition to being postracial. These politicians were as inspired by Bill Clinton and his ability to triangulate issues as they were by early practitioners of deracialization like Tom Bradley and Doug Wilder. In fact, appearing to transcend partisanship may actually help burnish a politician's postracial credentials. Showing some independence from the Democratic Party may help prove that a deracialized candidate is not beholden to traditional black interests, still heavily identified with the Democratic Party.

Postpartisanship, though, may be an even more difficult ideal to pursue than postracialism. While black candidates have ridden race-neutral platforms through the glass ceilings of high elective office in recent years, many scholars have opined that American politics is in an era of increasing party polarization. From the Tea Party forcing a rightward shift in the Republican Party to the high-profile defeats or retirements of many centrist Democratic and Republican members of Congress, there is often little incentive for politicians of either party to work across the aisle. Those who try may find their efforts thwarted and their electoral futures jeopardized.

Postpartisan politicians may also find themselves at odds with their partisan bases, just as deracialized politicians have sometimes found themselves at odds with African American constituents who seem to prefer some acknowledgment of racialized interests. If postpartisan politicians spend too much time trying to charm voters on the other end of the partisan or ideological spectrum, they may end up alienating more voters in their base than they gain on the other side.

As a rising presidential candidate in 2008, Barack Obama highlighted his bipartisan work as a Democratic state senator in a Republican-controlled legislature. He even touted his ethics work with conservative Senator Tom Coburn (R-OK) in the U.S. Senate. Since becoming President (and especially since Democrats lost control of the House), he has had to contend with a Republican caucus that is firm in its opposition to his agenda. Those experiences tempered President Obama's enthusiasm for bipartisanship and probably informed, to some degree, his willingness to exploit any weakness in Mitt Romney's background—even if it makes other Democrats a little queasy.

This grim reality of trying to govern and gain reelection in the most hyperpartisan environment in recent memory collided with Booker's rosy partisan transcendence when he spoke out about attack ads in May 2012. Booker could afford to be bipartisan because his electoral campaigns have heretofore been nonpartisan and his biggest political fights have been with other Democrats. Obama did not have that luxury;

he had to make a strongly partisan attack. The negative reaction from the left to Booker's comments, though, leaves many wondering if Booker can afford to be postpartisan much longer, either.

RECOMMENDED READING

Andra Gillespie (editor). 2009. *Whose Black Politics? Cases in Post-Racial Black Leadership*, London: Routledge. Provides a theoretical overview of young, deracialized, black politicians and illuminates their successes and challenges using case studies of ten leading black politicians of the 2000s.

Charles V. Hamilton. 1977. "De-Racialization: Examination of a Political Strategy," *First World* 1(2):3–5. Articulates Hamilton's original deracialization proposal.

Joseph McCormick II and Charles E. Jones. 1993. "The Conceptualization of Deracialization; Thinking through the Dilemma," in *Dilemmas of Black Politics* (pp. 66–84), edited by Georgia Pearsons. New York: Harper Collins. A chapter that outlines the normative implications of deracialization from a political science perspective.

Carol A. Pierannunzi and Jon D. Hutcheson. 1996. "The Rise and Fall of Deracialization: Andrew Young as Mayor and Gubernatorial Candidate," in *Race, Politics, and Governance in the United States* (pp. 96–106), edited by Huey L. Perry. Gainesville:

University Press of Florida. Uses the case study of Andrew Young's failed 1990 gubernatorial bid to highlight normative concerns with deracialized political candidates' balance between reaching out to non-black voters while maintaining strong relationships within the African American community.

Alexandra Starr. 2002. "We Shall Overcome, Too," *Business Week*, July 15. Provides a short synopsis of young black politicians and their neoliberal vision.

the sociology of silver

ANDREW LINDNER

n March 2012, close observers of the Republican presidential primary process were mystified by some of Rick Santorum's victories. The underdog candidate, known for his extreme social conservative politics, was not only doing relatively well compared to the much better-funded Mitt Romney, he was consistently performing better than polls predicted. In eleven heavily polled states, Santorum performed an average of 2.3% better than predicted by polling, even picking up unexpected victories in Alabama, Iowa, and Mississippi.

Puzzling over the results, Nate Silver crunched some numbers on his *New York Times*-hosted blog, FiveThirtyEight. To see whether other candidates were over- or underperforming, he produced a table with the average actual performance of each of the Republican candidates and their polling estimates in two different subsets of states. Silver hypothesized that the disparity might be explained by the underrepresentation of cell phone-only respondents who might skew toward

Santorum. Considering this possibility, he presented a chart examining the correlation between Santorum's performance and the percentage of cell phone-only polls. Unfortunately, the relationship was weak. Silver had to confess that he had no convincing answer to the mystery.

Still, the Santorum blog post illustrates Silver's *modus operandi*. He's been called a "statistical boy genius," a "numbers wizard," and a "hero to geeks" in his willingness to identify a question, seize on some data, and apply any and all statistical tools to answer it. He writes in straightforward, mercifully jargon-free prose, but like every good social scientist, Silver's chief devotion is to the findings, not to any particular ideology. In the always-risky field of political prediction, this approach has proven remarkably successful. On the eve of the 2008 presidential election, Silver correctly predicted forty-nine of fifty states and estimated the population vote within 0.4% of President Obama's 6.1% margin of victory.

And it's not just politics. Silver made his name as one of the original *Moneyball*-ers, developing the system of baseball player performance prediction known as PECOTA. More recently, he has created quality-of-life rankings for New York City neighborhoods, predicted Oscar and World Cup winners, and used online dating data to determine that Wednesday nights are optimal for "singles on the prowl." Silver's curiosity leads him to a wide variety of questions, and his process of answering those questions invariably uses statistical methods, traditionally the province of social scientists.

With his rapid-response blogging (he even live-tweeted the NBA Finals), Silver is clearly a man of his age. His versatile public intellectualism is hardly new. But compared to public intellectuals of the past, who benefited from widespread readership of serious nonfiction, Silver writes for a far narrower segment of highly engaged elites with relatively rarefied knowledge. As the American public intellectually disengages with civic life, the language of political discourse has become technocratic. To be sure, Silver is a democratizer of knowledge, but one whose public extends only as far as those with a semester of college stats under their belt. Today, to talk politics is to speak in statistics.

the changing marketplace of ideas

"Every year, 70 readers die and only 2 are replaced," novelist Philip Roth told journalist David Remnick in 2000. Roth's word choice was deliberate. In an age of e-mails, tweets, Facebook posts, and text messages, it's impossible to argue people aren't reading. What was and is fast becoming extinct is the *reader*, devoted to consuming and reflecting upon serious books. "Literature takes a habit of mind that has disappeared.

It requires silence, some form of isolation, and sustained concentration in the presence of an enigmatic thing," said Roth. Despite its many benefits for mental health and civil society, far fewer people are reading books than in the past. So, though Roth's invented numbers are hyperbolic, according to the National Endowment for the Arts, the percentage of American adults reading any kind of book without being assigned to do so declined from 67% in 1982 to 54% in 2008 (the most recent year of NEA's study). And if literature is in bad shape, the market for serious nonfiction is even worse. With the exception of a *Freakonomics* here or a *SuperFreakonomics* there, few Americans now read nonfiction informed by social scientific research or even rigorous journalism. While we must avoid the tendency to romanticize a great age of high-minded literacy that never quite was, it seems clear the audience for public intellectualism has shrunk.

At the same time, several other factors have converged to transform the nature of political discourse. As powerful computers have become widely available, social scientists have developed increasingly complex statistical methods, capable of analyzing dozens of models and tens of thousands of cases in seconds. This democratized access to computers has also helped statistics flourish in the same way it's spurred creativity in software development. At the same time twelve-year-old Mark Zuckerberg, future founder of Facebook, programmed video games in his parents' house in White Plains, eighteen-year-old Silver was running statistics software to beat his high school buddies in fantasy baseball.

Combined with expanded access to higher education, these factors contributed to the creation of a new technocratic elite. The segment of the public now interested in reading serious political analysis is more educated, more statistically literate, and more homogeneous. The marketplace of ideas has shrunk, and it now trades in more specialized goods.

According to the Archives of Internal Medicine, in 2010 just 24% of Americans can express 1 in 1,000 as a percentage. The Annie E. Casey Foundation revealed in 2002 that only 30% can correctly identify what "margin of error" means given four multiple-choice options. Yet Nate Silver regularly posts outputs from multivariate regression analyses, resplendent with unstandardized coefficients, standard errors, and $R2$s. These methods may seem like child's play for academics, but the percentage of the American population that can interpret such knowledge is minuscule. Even with his immense skill in translating statistics for the public, Silver merely expands his audience from the highly rarefied world of quantitative researchers to the only *somewhat* rarefied world of *New York Times* blog readers. And while the group that can grasp such specialized knowledge is small, Silver's technical, social scientific analysis has made him the toast (and inspiration) of the political class. In 2008, for example, the Obama campaign hosted a statistics training camp for campaign volunteers and, in 2012, Obama's reelection campaign hired a "data brigade" to produce predictive statistical models—the same type of analysis that changed baseball is changing politics.

If the content and the audience for public intellectualism has changed, so too has the medium. It's practically cliché to note that the slow, meditative form of the book has been replaced by the short, rapid-response media of tweets and blog posts. Magazine articles qualify as "long-form" analysis. Silver's primary outlet is his blog, but he also offers immediate reactions to breaking events by Twitter and more extensive analyses in media like the *New York Times Magazine.*

Silver exemplifies this form of Web-based, technocratic, public intellectualism. He's often called a "genius" for his ability to find clever ways to inform public debates with some nifty bit of data analysis. But, as Malcolm Gladwell tells us in *Outliers,* the term *genius* begs suspicion. Being smart is necessary, but not sufficient. Gladwell offers the example of Bill Gates, who achieved his fortune in part because of intelligence and passion, but also because of a series of highly unusual opportunities. Gates was born into a privileged background that allowed him access to 10,000 hours with computers at precisely the right moment in time.

The same is true for Silver. Born in 1978, Silver attended the University of Chicago in the late 1990s, a huge growth period for advanced statistics (remember, this is when fast, powerful, but compact computers had become publicly available). As a postgrad, he was at the perfect age to be among the vanguard of bloggers. Finally, he benefited from a historically rare level of public interest in the 2008 presidential election. Silver may have been the first to post Stata output on the *New York Times'* Web site, but if he hadn't, someone else surely would have.

Make no mistake, Silver is a very smart guy with a nose for useful data. My point is that he represents a mode of intellectualism that has resulted from major changes in the content, medium, and audience for political analysis. Had Edward R. Murrow turned 30 in 2008, he, too, might have tweeted about predictive models.

blogger sociology

Statistics are a tool. Statistical analysis has, for example, led to the creation of new financial instruments on Wall Street and more hi-tech methods of crime detection in police departments around the country. Still, there's much to bemoan about their immense influence in society, from their role in creating the exotic investments that led to the 2008 banking crisis to their potential to paint reductionist portraits of complex social circumstances. So, as we wouldn't despise the pencil, only the contemptible writer who put it to paper, there's nothing inherently wrong with statistical analysis. In Silver's case, his evenhanded use of statistics has nearly always enriched public debates with new sociological insights. At his best, Silver has the publishing speed and readability of journalism with the systematic evidence and complexity of academics. Silver's style indisputably reflects this freedom and great inventiveness in conjuring cleverly framed questions and elegant designs to answer them. His ethos might be: "Get an idea and a scrap of data. Publish the results in easily digested bites."

Unlike academics, Silver is unburdened by the constraining forces of peer review, turgid and esoteric disciplinary jargon, and the unwieldy format of academic manuscripts. He need not kowtow to past literature, offer exacting descriptions of his methods, or explain in tedious detail how his findings contribute to existing theory. The check on Silver's methods is, instead, his visibility. All his posts are immediately scrutinized by highly educated readers. In 2011, he began to acknowledge and often address these critiques in a regular post called "Reads and Reactions."

Unlike conventional journalists, he is not constrained by the "objectivity norm" or journalistic style. While most J-schools insist budding reporters keep themselves out of the story, one of the great pleasures of Silver's work is his original analysis and perspective. Unafraid to admit political opinions, he establishes credibility with his commitment to empirical evidence. As a blogger, he can write his own style guide.

In these ways, Silver has developed his own sociology, exploring social divisions, challenging "commonsense" assumptions with evidence, and critiquing social scientific methods. For example, one of Silver's long-term projects (an interest shared by many academics) is to better understand the ways in which Americans are divided, particularly in political preferences. In a postelection think piece in *Esquire*, Silver wrote, "If Bill Clinton was the first black president, then Barack Obama might be the first urban one." He went on to explain that, since at least the late 1980s, rural areas have favored Republicans and urban areas have tilted Democratic. But in 2008, Obama saw a 10.5 million-vote margin of victory in urban areas, while McCain had a significant edge in rural areas. This difference, Silver explained, wasn't simply a function of the disproportionate number of black and young voters in urban areas—white and older urban people disproportionately voted for Obama, too. With more people living in cities than in rural areas, Obama's victory was virtually guaranteed. Instead, Obama won urban areas by such a lopsided margin in part because his identity was, Silver said, "unmistakably urban: pragmatic, superior, hip, stubborn, multicultural." All the symbols that appealed to an urban voting public—Obama's education, race, fluency with pop culture—represented a cultural threat to the orthodox worldview in rural areas. More importantly, urban voters tend to lean Democratic and there were more urban voters than ever before.

This fairly simple analysis of voting data allowed Nate Silver to catch an important voting cleavage many pundits missed. The results of the 2008 election weren't determined by facts unique to this political race (that is, that black voters wanted a black president or young voters liked Jay-Z references). The results emerged from long-term demographic shifts.

For Silver, such divisions of race, class, gender, age, education, and urbanity are crucial to understanding the American political landscape. His phenomenal success in predicting the outcomes of the 2008 Democratic primary and, later, the general election was built on a statistical formula that modeled the demographic characteristics of various voting districts. In this way, he could tell that districts with older, more female voters would lean heavily toward Hillary Clinton. A model that combined factors of age, education, race, and gender with current polling produced far better predictions than polling data alone.

Understanding the consequences of social divisions is essential to Silver's brand of political sociology, but so is challenging conventional wisdom with empirical evidence. Among the most popular political assumptions is former Clinton adviser James Carville's assertion "It's the economy, stupid." For Carville, this conviction stems from a gut-level response to his personal experiences on the campaign trail—elections are won because of economics. For Silver, this is a testable question.

In November 2011, Silver posted a blog analyzing which of 43 economic measures (from Consumer Price Index to Change in Nonfarm Payrolls) best predicts the popular vote in presidential elections. Contrary to Carville's view, Silver found no economic measure could explain more than 46% of the popular vote in elections between 1948 and 2008. In response, for the 2012 presidential election, Silver developed state-level models that combine polling averages, previous presidential election results, and state demographics. These results are aggregated into a national model and combined with economic measures. Using this model, which incorporates economic factors as well as social and political characteristics, Silver then runs 10,000 simulated election outcomes. As of mid-June 2012, Silver's model showed Obama winning in 63% of these simulated elections. The end result of Silver's work is increasing the complexity of political debate by overturning poor assumptions and offering sophisticated alternatives.

Silver's skepticism over the predictive power of "economic fundamentals" also speaks to a final characteristic of his approach to statistical analysis of society. He is deeply humble about the limitations of prediction. Like all good social scientists, Silver tends to hammer away about these limitations, even as readers drool in anticipation of his next forecasting model. In March 2012, he warned "... we can get into trouble when we exaggerate how much we know about the future. Although election forecasting is a relatively obscure topic, you'll see the same mistakes in fields like finance and earthquake prediction in which the stakes are much higher."

the dangers of statistics

Despite the obvious value of statistics for advancing public debate, there are serious problems with this mode of public intellectualism. Silver's methodology is inherently exclusive. He's a brilliant translator of statistical ideas into more accessible terms, but statistics remain a form of elite knowledge. So, if the weakness of most journalistic coverage of politics and social issues is a lack of technical precision and sophistication, its core strength was its ability to connect with a broad audience. Silver's model has the opposite problem: It excludes all but elite readers. Paul Krugman, a Nobel Prize-winning economist and Silver's colleague at the *New*

York Times, seems aware of this boundary. When one of his blog posts is fairly technical or statistical, Krugman appends the title with "(wonky)." In doing so, Krugman warns that all who tread here must come armed with a fluency in the language of statistics and economics.

Of course, readers need not follow such links, and they can certainly skip the confusing bits of Silver's posts. When they do so, however, the gap in knowledge between elites and the rest of the public widens. Perhaps more tellingly, the bigger divide goes beyond those who do (and do not) read Krugman and Silver's blogs—it's the gap between blog readers and the general readers of yesteryear, most of whom are no longer reading books, never mind statistically oriented blogs.

Like it or not, statistics are an essential part of public discourse. Those without proficiency are at a disadvantage. Given the widespread lack of understanding, statistics (invented or otherwise) can be easily manipulated by elites. In the official Republican response to President Obama's 2012 State of the Union address, for example, Indiana governor Mitch Daniels depicted unemployment as dire, noting that "nearly half of persons under 30 did not go to work today." In one sense, Daniels's statement was true (well, close: It was actually 44.4%). However, the statement is deceptive because it includes people ages 16 to 22, many of whom are in high school or college. For people ages 25 to 29 in the labor market, the correct number at the time was closer to 9.7%—high, but not *half*. Most Americans lack the statistical proficiency to identify the error and know how to find the actual rate. This sort of statistical deception is par for the course in public life today.

The role of public intellectuals of the past was to stand as a bulwark against powerful individuals and institutions by informing the public. Today, Nate Silver's application of sophisticated statistical tools in accessible, readable ways continues in this watchdog tradition. At the same time, the statistical nature of contemporary political analysis like Silver's has the potential to widen the gap between the haves and have-nots in their ability to fully participate in democratic society.

RECOMMENDED READING

Nate Silver's Greatest Hits:

- 2009. "How Obama Really Won the Election," *Esquire*, January 14.
- 2009. "Oscar Predictions You Can Bet On! Mr. Statistics, Nate Silver, Goes for the Gold," *New York Magazine*, February 15.
- 2010. "The Most Livable Neighborhoods in New York: A Quantitative Index of the 50 Most Satisfying Places to Live," *New York Magazine*, April 11.

- 2012. "Election Forecast: Obama Begins with Tenuous Advantage," *New York Times* Blog FiveThirtyEight, June 7.
- 2012. "Models Based on 'Fundamentals' Have Failed at Predicting Presidential Elections," *New York Times* Blog FiveThirtyEight, March 26.
- 2012. *The Signal and the Noise: Why So Many Predictions Fail—But Some Don't*, New York: Penguin Books.

Other Resources:

Joel Best. 2001. *Damned Lies and Statistics: Untangling Numbers from the Media, Politicians, and Activists*, Berkeley: University of California Press. Best has made a career of pointing out the ways people lie with statistics and helping readers develop the statistical literacy to spot such fibs.

Caleb Crain. 2007. "Twilight of the Books: What Will Life Be Like If People Stop Reading," *The New Yorker*, December 24. A widely read reflection on the decline in reading (and its consequences for the way we think).

Kaiser Fung. 2010. *Numbers Rule Your World: The Hidden Influence of Probabilities and Statistics on Everything You Do*, New York: McGraw-Hill Professional. Describes the many exciting, disturbing, and often invisible ways the world is run by statistical information.

Michael Lewis. 2003. *Moneyball: The Art of Winning an Unfair Game*, New York: Norton. The most fascinating book ever written about statistics, this tome explains how stats took over the American pastime.

joe soss on american poverty governance, as it is and as it might be

SARAH SHANNON

*T*he Office Hours podcasts are among the most popular content on The Society Pages. In this installment, Sarah Shannon talks with Joe Soss, the Cowles Chair for the Study of Public Service at the University of Minnesota's Humphrey School of Public Affairs and author, with Richard C. Fording and Sanford F. Schram, of the book Disciplining the Poor: Neoliberal Paternalism and the Persistent Power of Race (2011, University of Chicago Press). *The full audio interview is available at* the societypages.org/politics.

In this conversation, as in his new book, Joe Soss traces the tremendous continuities, as well as the major changes that have occurred in welfare provision and poverty governance in the United States over the past forty years. In particular, we take on how racial, political, and economic factors have shaped welfare policies in the United States and how, to address poverty in the long run, we may need more democracy.

Sarah Shannon: Joe, you have a new book: *Disciplining the Poor*. How did you get started on this project?

Joe Soss: The initial idea, actually, for the project was that we were just going to try and look at some issues around how this new approach to dealing with poverty in the United States was operating on the ground. And so the project really started in a bottom-up way. We wanted to get some administrative data and also go do some field visits to look in the state of Florida, which was pursuing a strong form of the new approach to poverty governance, to really look at what was going on down there and how things were operating. Because we all shared an interest in race and its role in poverty politics, we were particularly interested in how race operated within that new system. And once we began to analyze the administrative data, we began to see a lot of things that resonated with some of the other work that we were doing and had done that we weren't thinking of as part of the same thing, really, but it was on why states were choosing the policies they were and what was going on nationally with public opinion. And we began to see a much larger and more coherent story coming together: There seemed to be the same sorts of things operating in similar ways at different levels of the system. Eventually, after working on several pieces on this and different articles, we decided to step back and turn it into a book project.

Shannon: "Neoliberal paternalism" is really important for understanding your book's argument. Can you explain what it is?

Soss: Yeah, so we use this term *neoliberal paternalism*, which we're not the first to have used (there are other scholars who have as well), but we define it in a particular way that I think is important. Essentially, our argument is that if you want to understand the direction of historical change in poverty governance in the United States, you have to see it as occurring at the intersection of two movements that have changed policy and politics. One is neoliberalism, which is a form of what we call "market fundamentalism." In many ways, it places the state and lots of other social relations in a subordinate position to the market. It's really about changing the way in which the state carries out its business, reorganizing the state itself around market principles, and redirecting the state to actually serve market needs in various ways. So, today we see that the state is used to open up markets, it's used to construct markets, it's used to absorb market losses (like through the bailouts and a variety of other issues that are currently very controversial in terms of the Occupy Wall Street movement)—the state is far from pulling *back* from its obligations and, in terms of being active in the economy, has expanded its activities. So, the state is actively involved, for the poor, in attempting to move people into the market, in attempting to immerse people in market experiences so that they will "learn" to conduct themselves in ways that are needed to be employees. It sort of builds these classes for people and creates incentives for people to go into the market.

Paternalism arose at the same time, in a sense, as the reform movement in poverty governance. As the name suggests, paternalism's really modeled on the traditional father-child authority relationship. The idea that the father has an obligation to guide and help the child, because children, in a sense, are not able to recognize what's in their best interests—or, if they recognize it, do not have the self-discipline to bring their behavior in line with their good intentions. And so the father, at various times, needs to set the agenda for what the child needs to do. In this view, the state needs to punish behavior that deviates from expectations, needs to reward and incentivize better behavior, needs to monitor behavior at all times . . .

Its domestic side is equally important, and it really has been an important part of the movement to shift poverty governance toward a model where the state is seen as having a fundamental responsibility to cultivate social order, to ensure social order in poor communities, and to also instill discipline in individuals from those communities. We see this rise of paternalism in the criminal justice system and the rise of mass incarceration in the United States, in the variety of changes in policing and criminal justice, and also on the welfare side, wherein we see a new model of providing aid on the basis of expectations, monitoring, and then meting out penalties for noncompliance and incentives for compliance.

Shannon: You use a particular model for looking at race—the "racial classification model of policy choice"—talk a little bit about that model and how you use it, maybe both as you're looking at things at the national, historical level, but then also how you saw race operating on the ground.

Soss: There's a real problem here of trying to understand how it is that we can observe such tremendous racial inequalities and racial disparities in treatment under the cover of official public policy in an era in which it is *illegal* to make racial distinctions and design different types of treatment for different groups in the letter of the law, in an era in which the vast majority of the people in the United States tend to endorse, at least on the surface, norms of racial equality. Our approach to understanding this is to begin from the premise that, really, it's not explained by that old image that people like to fall back on (which still has some truth to it, and there are many instances where there's a problem), but that sort of white people who have conscious prejudice and, in a sense, intentionally discriminate against people who are not part of their own group—a kind of conscious "us-them" dynamic, favoring those who are part of your own racial group or ethnic group and acting negatively toward those who threaten you as the out-group. That just doesn't explain things very well in the context we're looking at.

So what's going on? Well, we take what we understand to be a basically structural view of race. We begin from the idea that race operates in a way that it structures social relations. It's an important part of our politics, for example, people's understandings of the parties and the kind of competition that we see between the political parties in the United States is aligned with the racial dimension of politics. The Democratic Party and the Republican Party are understood as having different positions on race, racial policy issues, and also on many of the social problems that people associate with, for example, the "urban underclass." And so race, not only in terms of who votes for whom but also in terms of the very structure of competition in our politics, just as one example, is structured around race. The economy also. Economic relations are structured in important ways around race, because race matters so greatly for where people live, the extent to which they're segregated in where they live, the kind of education and human capital they acquire, and the kind of opportunities they have available to them in the market—we have, in many ways, racially structured labor markets.

So, because race matters so much for political relations and economic relations, it is, in a sense, *inevitable* that race will matter for the set of institutions that govern policy. That in a sense, race is just a creature of our political and economic life together. It's constructed and will always, to some degree, reflect those relations. To the extent that race structures those relations, it's going to matter for poverty governance as well.

But at the same time that we think you have to deal with race as a social structure, you also have to ask, "How is it that race actually affects the way people think about these issues, the decisions people make, and the actions they take?" Because, ultimately, the outcomes we get are not simply pure products of social structure.

Human agency matters a lot; people act within those social structures, but they're not determined in how they act.

Shannon: They're not robots!

Soss: Yeah, they're not robots. And so we want to understand how race ultimately matters. And if we're saying that we can't really understand that well through a model of intentional discrimination and prejudice, what's going on?

The argument we make is that, when people attempt to design or implement policy, they tend to do so in a way where they think about the actors that they're applying the policy to and try to figure out what might work. And that their impressions about what *might* work: "Is this a group that isn't doing what we want because they don't have the opportunity?" or "Is this a group that isn't doing what we want because they don't have the motivation and they need incentives to do it?" or "Is this a group that would only respond to threats and punishments?" or . . . that as people look at the groups, they have limited information about those groups. One of the things they often have access to is racial information. They can identify that we're talking about a primarily Latina group here, right, or an African American group, or they know the race or ethnicity of the person that they're dealing with in an administrative setting. And that they use a kind of what psychologists call "heuristic reasoning," in that they take the small amounts of information they have and extrapolate from that. They "fill in the details" in some sense.

And our model basically draws on a set of research that comes from psychology and sociology that is often referred to as "implicit racism theory" or "implicit cognitive theory," and it suggests that a lot of this goes on behind the curtain. People are not aware that they're doing this in many cases, but they look at who they're designing policy for, implementing it for, and they make judgments about what is needed. They make judgments about (in implementation settings) whether a certain behavior indicates a real problem or is a one-time thing. There's nothing wrong with making those judgments, but race is a potential basis for those judgments. And we argue that, in some cases more than others, we see racial biases emerge in judgments.

You asked about the implementation setting. So, you know, a good example here is that some people may be aware of some work that Devah Pager, a sociologist, did where she looked at the interplay of race and a felony drug conviction on the likelihood that someone would be hired for a job. What she found was, if you had people going out and applying for a job who were identical except some were white and some black, and then among those, one white person (male) had a criminal conviction and one did not and one black male had a conviction and one did not, the biggest effect in terms of not getting hired was when you attached the criminal conviction (that discrediting marker) to the African American male.

And we drew from that the idea that it's important to think about race as a source of vulnerability. It's not always the case that white clients and black clients in a welfare program are going to be treated differently, but under certain conditions that will emerge strongly. And our classification model is an attempt to specify those conditions. So, for example, we found in an experiment with case managers, and corroborated this with administrative data, that when you attach to someone's record (first in a hypothetical vignette, then in the actual administrative vignette) a note saying that this person has a prior sanction, that it has no discernible, statistical effect on the likelihood that a white client will be sanctioned. White clients would not be sanctioned at a greater rate just because they had that prior sanction on their record. But for black clients, we find a *tremendous* increase in the likelihood that they'll be sanctioned.

Or, to take another example, people are sanctioned (that is, penalties are applied to them in welfare programs) more often in politically conservative regions than in politically liberal regions. But when you look at data from public opinion surveys in the United States, what you find is that negative stereotypes of African Americans (and, to some extent, Latinos) relative to white Americans run much higher among conservatives than among liberals. So the implication we draw from that is that the effect of shifting from being in a liberal region to a conservative region should be much greater for minority clients, and, in fact, that is what we find. For white clients, it doesn't really matter that much whether they pursue welfare benefits in a very conservative region or a very liberal region, but for black clients in particular, we see a very large increase in the likelihood of being sanctioned when they move to a conservative region.

One last example is one of the great racialized stereotypes of welfare in the United States: the idea that poor African Americans are more likely to *prefer* to stay on welfare for a long period of time and "avoid work," in some sense, relative to white Americans. Taking that aspect of racial difference, we hypothesize that the longer people's spells become—the longer they stay in the welfare program—the more that gap should emerge between the rates at which white clients are sanctioned and black clients are sanctioned. In fact, that's just what we find. The differences are quite small (and even statistically insignificant) in the first months, but by the time you get out toward a year of participation in a welfare program, this gap has emerged, with black clients *much* more likely to get sanctioned than white clients. We think, again, consistent with the other findings, this is because, in a sense, their record gives a stereotype-consistent cue that seems to confirm the expectation that this person will be a "problem" in some sense. They now look like the long-term welfare recipient of stereotyping more, much like the person who has a prior sanction on their record now looks like more of a problem client if they're a person of color.

Shannon: To finish, could you please talk a bit about your policy suggestions and today's interesting political climate?

Soss: Sure! I'll try to be brief. There's no magic policy design, there's no way to design a policy that is going to serve low-income people well so long as we don't deal with the underlying issues about the sort of weakening of democracy in the United States, the racial dimensions of our politics, the gender dimensions—all these sorts of things. And there's no way to design good poverty policies, really, that are going to overcome problems in the market unless we deal with the fact that jobs are not designed to allow for caring obligations: Bad poverty policies can be bad under *any* circumstances, but good poverty policies can only be as good as the underlying social relations that they serve. So we really can't divorce the effort to change poverty policy and poverty governance from the kind of broad efforts at reform that we see in the Occupy Wall Street Movements today, various things like that. We have to understand that these are intimately related, and you really have to deal with the whole.

But within that, I think we kind of owe it to the readers, after taking them through this long critical analysis, to offer some ideas about what better policies would look like. Much of what we argue is that there are certain aspects of what's wrong with the current system that really *can* be improved through central, national policies, through national control. For example, a lot of the racial inequalities that we observe would not be possible without a devolved system of federalism, in which choices are being made in different places according to the racial characteristics of their populations. We also think there are a lot of dynamics that suggest that benefits levels ought to be set at the federal level for the poor. There ought to be, you know, federal child care policies and transportation policies to assist people in various ways, but that ultimately our argument is that federalism really can play an important role and localism can play an important role, even though we observe mainly negative effects from those things in the book. We think it's the way it's been designed, not necessarily inherent to the system. So what we argue at the end of the book is that we need to have meaningful federal floors, whether it be minimum wage laws or federal benefit levels for the poor for assistance or various service systems and supports, but that states should be able to rise *above* those floors and attempt to provide greater services and supports in various ways (but not fall below it). Once you establish those sort of foundations at the federal level, there's also a set of issues that really can be handled at the local level and *should* be, because people want to be able to have the opportunity to govern themselves in different ways in different localities, different states. But the argument that we make is that ultimately, like many of the problems having to do with the financial crisis and many of the issues that are at the heart of the protest movements right now, are actually much like the problems in the poverty governance problems of democracy. They're problems of insufficient democratization.

And we argue, in many respects, rather than the sort of top-down paternalist imposition of expectations and incentives and punishments, we really need to think about poverty programs as being a site where people are really addressing the most fundamental issues in their lives. The clients have a lot to say about what their problems are, they have a lot to add to the discussion of what kinds of benefits they need individually and what their communities need in order to flourish. We really need to design programs around a much more democratic set of values that draws people into the process. I think the evidence shows, actually, that when you have program designs like that, people actually benefit from them.

One of the things I've studied in the past is the contrast between cash welfare programs, which have these very paternalist designs, and Head Start programs, which have these participatory parents' councils in which people have obligations to join together to talk about how the center is going to be run for their children. What I find, of course (even though Head Start is in many ways designed for the children), is that people (parents who become involved in these participatory councils in the Head Start programs) have higher involvement levels of civic engagement and political engagement as a result. And also, they actually do better economically—there tend to be positive effects on their outcomes in the labor market as well. So, in some ways, giving people obligations that empower them is very different from and more positive than the kind of "responsibility" that paternalists have argued for—that is, simply making people responsible for failing to meet the expectations that are being set from above. It's a different notion of responsibility.

We argue for a system in which we start with broad reforms in terms of political and economic relations, then attempt to establish various federal floors that guarantee people certain necessary support in order to improve their lives, and then allow for certain types of local control that would let people to participate in the democratic process of the authority being exercised over their lives. But ultimately, there is no way to deal with poverty in the United States until we reform the kind of jobs that are available to people with low skill levels. Until we change economic relations so people can have access to jobs that offer wages they can live on, that offer the benefits that they need and their children and their parents need, that offer the kinds of flexibility that allow for care work, we're not going to have a good fit between the realities of people's lives and the labor market.

TSP tie-in

sexism, politics,
and the media

Women in power face a sexist double bind in which they cannot be too "masculine" (and risk being labeled a "bitch") or too "feminine" (and risk losing respect). Even *hypothetical* female leaders who are painted as powerful or strong willed have their very womanhood and femininity questioned and undermined (browse to thesocietypages.org/politics for links to a post that explores this dynamic in a popular film). The media often focuses on female leaders' bodies and personal style. Most recently, high-profile political players Sarah Palin, Hillary Clinton, and Michelle Obama have all been subject to such bodily scrutiny. The Society Pages' Community Page Sociological Images has collected multiple examples in which female politicians' appearances have made headlines. For example, Michelle Obama has consistently had articles written about her sartorial choices—including her willingness to wear "bargain brands" and wear the same outfit several times—and her body, especially her arms. While Obama has made a point of insisting on talking about her contributions, not her looks, it's interesting to note that the narrative about her personal style has actually displaced an earlier narrative, in which she was highly criticized in her husband's first presidential campaign. In 2007 and 2008, Obama was seen too independent, too career focused (that is, on her career, not her husband's), and too aggressive. She was drawn literally and metaphorically as a stereotypical "angry black woman," lampooned as a radical Angela Davis acolyte too dangerous for the White House.

During *her* run for vice president in 2008, then-Governor of Alaska Sarah Palin was often sexualized and trivialized—an accomplished politician minimized with terms like "Caribou Barbie." Sociologists have long documented how sexualizing a woman is a way to make her seem less powerful, less important. Portrayals like Palin's November 2009 *Newsweek* cover, which showed her in pigtails, tell the viewer that women like this are not to be taken seriously. Additionally, Palin's political success was often attributed in the media and by rivals as owing entirely to her embrace of a feminized portrayal. Former Secretary of State Hillary Clinton, on the other hand, has often been criticized for *not* being glamorous. In fact, Clinton has faced possibly the most hateful media sexism in recent years, being portrayed as "bitchy," "shrill," "mannish," and physically unappealing. These comments usually come in the form *gender policing*, a process by which the subject is portrayed as not fitting the norms of their gender. Here, Clinton is portrayed as overly masculine and is reminded in a belittling way to get back to feminine duties— which include, in a heteronormative narrative, being visually pleasing to the opposite sex and, if a sign held up at a Clinton event in 2008 is any indication, ironing a man's shirt (again, see thesocietypages.org/politics for links).

How does such sexism affect women considering running for political office or working toward leadership positions in companies, at universities, and in their communities? Are they held back or discouraged by the sexism leveled at their predecessors? The first woman was elected to Congress in 1917, but as seen on the Graphic Sociology blog, their proportion of representation has risen to just 20% today. This is a significantly smaller percentage than other rich countries— for instance, Sweden's parliament is fully half female. Around the world, twenty countries have female presidents or prime ministers, but in the United States the sexism female politicians are faced with on the campaign trail may be holding them back.

KIA HEISE

discussion guide and group activities

discussion guide

1. In the Introduction, the editors explain that, when it comes to the study of politics, sociology has tools that differentiate it from other disciplines, like political science. Choose one chapter from this volume and explain what is sociological about the approach taken by the author(s). How does sociology contribute to understanding the political phenomenon analyzed in the chapter?

2. Today, one of the most powerful actors is the state. Where does the state's power come from? In the essay by Vincent J. Roscigno (Chapter 1), you read about Max Weber's three categories of authority. Choose a well-known leader and discuss which type of authority you believe he or she draws upon. Do those in your reading group agree?

3. Several chapters within this volume deal specifically with the relationship between race and politics. Why do

you think this is the case? What other connections between the two do you think are important for the American election process?

4. Browse to thesocietypages.org/politics to listen to Chapter 11's author, Enid Logan, give an interview about the politics of race. What, according to Logan, are the *new* politics of race, and what makes them new? How do other social categories, like gender, age, or religion, impact candidates' (and our) lives, and how do they work together?

5. The essays in this volume highlight how technology is tightly linked to the political landscape, from Facebook to *The Daily Show*. Browse to thesocietypages.org/politics to read the Cyborgology piece "Presidential Debates: The Social Medium Is the Message." How have Americans moved beyond the passive consumption of political knowledge, and how does this help or hinder the political process? Drawing on the essay by Jose Marichal (Chapter 8), what is the relationship between Facebook and political participation? For those with experience or knowledge in other countries, how does this relationship vary internationally?

6. As Steven Buechler's essay (Chapter 4) highlights, many citizens become involved with political issues through social movements. Read the TSP Roundtable "Social

Scientists Studying Social Movements," found at thesocietypages.org/politics. Considering the contributors' insights, think about a social movement you'd like to study. Why do you want to know more? How could you best get the information you're looking for?

7. Politics isn't just about the government. Instead, as you read in Chapters 6, 7, and 9, it touches many facets of social life. Think of something (other than sports or religion) that isn't traditionally thought of as political and provide an example of how it can be politicized as well as how it can impact politics.

8. "Democracy" is a key concept in Chapters 4, 8, and others. What *is* democracy? Spend a few minutes writing your own definition. Then, find an image that you think represents this definition. If you get stuck, check out the TSP Community Page Sociological Images at thesocietypages.org/socimages.

9. Browse thesocietypages.org/politics to find a Graphic Sociology post titled "Congressional Demographics." Why do you think the women accounted for less than 20% of the 112th Congress? Taking a global view, choose three countries and conduct some research to see what percentage of their legislatures are composed of women. How do these countries compare in gender representation to the United States?

10. Chapter 14 shows some of the promise of social policy to effect change. Think of a social issue that you care about; can you think of a policy that could address this issue?

group activities

FEATURED GROUP ACTIVITY 1: POWER

As the essay by Vincent J. Roscigno (Chapter 1) shows, you can't discuss politics without discussing power. The activity below brings conceptions of power to the forefront.

Guidelines for the Facilitator

1. Make four signs labeled "agree," "strongly agree," "disagree," and "strongly disagree." Hang one sign in each corner of the room.
2. Tell participants that you will be reading a series of statements about power. After you read the first of the statements on page 217, participants should stand under the sign that most closely reflects their reaction to the statement.
3. After participants have assembled under the signs, ask each group to discuss why they picked that particular position and to choose a spokesperson to explain their position.
4. After each group gives their position, ask participants to return to the center of the room, then again go to stand

under the sign that most closely reflects their own reaction to the statement. (This gives participants the opportunity to change their positions if they wish.) Ask a few volunteers to explain whether and why they decided to change their positions.

5. Repeat this exercise for each statement. You can add or subtract statements to alter the length of the exercise.

Statements About Power

- "Power corrupts."
- "You can't get anything done without power."
- "Power is connected to race" (you could also ask about class, gender, etc.).
- "People or organizations that want to change things in their community should seek power."

FEATURED ACTIVITY 2: SOCIAL STATISTICS

Many people do not realize that social science, even statistics, is everywhere in the form of political polls. As Chapters 2 and 13 explain, asking questions, conveying results, and interpreting data isn't as easy as we'd like to think. The quick activity below makes this point and brings methodology into the discussions on politics.

Guidelines for the Facilitator

Have the group brainstorm a topic and audience for a fictitious political poll. Participants could choose a real issue in a current election, but it isn't necessary. Then, have the participants form small groups. Each group should develop three questions about the topic. After ten minutes ask each group to share their questions. Discuss the type and effectiveness of the "survey" questions by asking:

- Are they closed or open-ended and why might this matter?
- What do they measure?
- How are they different?
- Are there ambiguous words, jargon, or other confusing items in any of the questions?
- How would a different target audience change the way the questions must be written?
- How would you represent the results?

about the contributors

Hollie Nyseth Brehm is a PhD candidate in sociology at the University of Minnesota. She studies human rights, international crime, and environmental sociology.

Steven Buechler is in the department of sociology at Minnesota State University, Mankato. He is the author of *Understanding Social Movements: Theories from the Classical Era to the Present* (2011, Paradigm Publishers).

Deborah Carr is in the sociology department and the Institute for Health, Health Care Policy, and Aging Research at Rutgers University. She is the coauthor of *Introduction to Sociology* (W. W. Norton & Company), now in its 8th edition.

Sinan Erensu is in the sociology program at the University of Minnesota. He studies social movements.

Joe R. Feagin is in the department of sociology at Texas A&M University. He is the author of *Systemic Racism: A Theory of Oppression* (2006, Routledge).

Corey Fields is in the department of sociology at Stanford University. He studies race and the role of identity in structuring social life.

Joseph Gerteis is in the sociology department at the University of Minnesota. He studies the dynamics of difference and solidarity, and he is the author of *Class and the Color Line* (2007, Duke University Press Books).

Andra Gillespie is in political science at Emory University. She is the editor of and a contributor to *The New Black Politician: Cory Booker, Newark, and Post-Racial America* (2012, New York University Press).

Kyle Green is in the sociology program at the University of Minnesota. He studies gender, sport, the body, and ritual.

Douglas Hartmann is in the sociology department at the University of Minnesota. His research interests focus on race and ethnicity, multiculturalism, popular culture (including sports and religion), and contemporary American society. He is the coeditor of The Society Pages.

Kia Heise is in the sociology program at the University of Minnesota. She studies social movements and race relations.

Wing Young Huie is an award-winning documentary photographer and author who lives in Minneapolis, Minnesota.

Sarah Lageson is in the sociology program at the University of Minnesota. She studies media, crime, and law. Lageson is a cohost of the Office Hours podcast on The Society Pages.

Andrew Lindner is in the sociology and social work department at Concordia College in Moorhead, Minnesota. He studies social theory, stratification, and the intersections of politics and the mass media.

Enid Logan is in the department of sociology at the University of Minnesota. She is the author of *"At This Defining Moment": Barack Obama's Presidential Candidacy and the New Politics of Race* (2011, New York University Press).

Jose Marichal is in the department of political science at California Lutheran University. He is the author of *Facebook*

Democracy (2012, Ashgate) and he is a blogger for The Society Pages' Community Page ThickCulture.

Vincent J. Roscigno is in the sociology department at The Ohio State University. He is the author of *The Face of Discrimination: How Race and Gender Impact Work and Home Lives* (2007, Rowman & Littlefield Publishers).

Sarah Shannon is in the department of sociology at the University of Georgia. She studies law, crime, and deviance and says that, like Chuck D., she'd like to reach the bourgeois and rock the boulevard.

Christopher Uggen is in the sociology department at the University of Minnesota. He studies crime, law, and deviance, especially how former prisoners manage to put their lives back together. He is the coeditor of The Society Pages.

index